More Advance Praise for *Womanish*

"Full of feeling and absorbing incident, Kim McLarin's *Womanish* is a companion book for searchers of the soul. In the tradition of James Baldwin, Alice Walker, and Henry Thoreau, McLarin's essays reveal an original mind in action and set to take action. Read *Womanish* to be inspired, to get angry, and to learn to hold and use that anger in our incendiary times."
—**MEGAN MARSHALL**, Pulitzer Prize-winning author of *Margaret Fuller: A New American Life* and *Elizabeth Bishop: A Miracle for Breakfast*

"Bold, well-crafted essays on living, loving, and striving while black."—***KIRKUS REVIEWS***

"*Womanish* is the education the United States needs but doesn't deserve. Not only has McLarin done the homework, she's created an elegant cheat sheet in the form of thirteen perfect essays."
—***FOREWORD*** (starred review)

WOMANISH

*A Grown Black Woman Speaks
on Love and Life*

Kim McLarin

PUBLISHING

New York, NY

Printed in the United States of America.
10 9 8 7 6 5 4 3 2 1

Ig Publishing
Box 2547
New York, NY 10163
www.igpub.com

ISB: ISBN: 978-1-632460-79-0 (paperback)

CONTENTS

Womanist (Opp. of "girlish," i.e. frivolous, irresponsible, not serious). A Black feminist or feminist of color. From the Black folk expression of mothers to female children, "you acting **womanish**," i.e., like a woman. Usually referring to outrageous, audacious, courageous or *willful* behavior. Wanting to know more and in greater depth than is considered "good" for one. Interested in grown up doings. Acting grown up. Being grown up. Interchangeable with another Black folk expression: "You trying to be grown." Responsible. In charge. *Serious.*

Alice Walker,
In Search of Our Mothers' Gardens: Womanist Prose

ACKNOWLEDGEMENTS

"Victim and Victor Both Start With V" appeared first in *themorningnews.org* as "Moving Stars."

"A Case for Revenge" appeared first as "The Low Road" in *themorningnews.org*.

"Eshu Finds Work" appeared first in *The New England Review*

"Maurice's Blues" first appeared in *The Sewanee Review*

The author is grateful to these publications for permission to reprint these essays.

Disclaimer: Some names and identifying details have been changed to protect the privacy of individuals.

Womanish

Alright, Cupid

When we have pleaded for understanding, our character has been distorted; when we have asked for simple caring, we have been handed empty inspirational appellations, then stuck in a far corner. When we have asked for love, we have been given children. In short, even our plainer gifts, our labors of fidelity and love, have been knocked down our throats.

—Alice Walker, "In Search of Our Mothers' Gardens," 1974

The first step of deprogramming is education, informing the person you are trying to free just how indoctrination works to hamstring a mind. But information alone will not free a believer from her beliefs, no matter how destructive, because belief is not intellectual. Emotion got you in and emotion will get you out.

By the time I stepped into online dating, I knew a great deal about the corrosive internalized effects of white supremacy and anti-Black bias. I knew about the old doll test[1] and the new doll test[2] and the Implicit Bias data showing 50 percent of Black people prefer white faces over Black. I knew that even as dark-skinned Black women evidence remarkable levels of self-esteem, colorism remains alive and well in the Black community. I even knew, after not-insignificant therapy, that I was kind and intelligent and compassionate and also, by the way, beautiful—and that nothing American society had been whispering in my ear should stand in the way of my feeling worthy of love.

I also knew that it did.

What I needed, it turned out, was a cheap, effective, powerful tool for deprogramming myself of the belief—partly personal, mostly hegemonic—in my own unlovability, a tool of liberation and empowerment, one that worked on both mind and heart. Audre Lorde famously wrote that the master's tools would never dismantle the master's house, but what I needed was to first dismantle the shack the master had built for me, and then to build myself a new home, brick by brick. Using, you know, the tools I had.

This is where online dating comes in.

•

These are the lessons I learned from online dating:

    I. Declaring that you want to be loved is empowering.
    II. Seeing how many people want to love you as you are is
        empowering.
    III. Understanding the choice is yours is empowering.

I.

After her divorce, my mother never dated. In part this was because she had four young daughters (and one young son) to protect and knew well the dangers of leaving unknown men lying around the house. But she also believed (not unreasonably, given her experience) that men were more trouble than they were worth.

That a woman is complete unto herself and does not need a man (or any partner) to live a rich, fulfilling life is a truth that begs the question: the issue is not need but want. A lot of straight women I know "don't want to be bothered" and though some of my friends in this category are white the majority of them are Black. *I can't be bothered*, they say as I recall my latest dating disaster. *I can't be bothered*, they say as I cry about a broken heart. *I can't be bothered*, they say and I hear, beneath the personal declaration, a judgment, an implication that continuing to want to be bothered reveals some major weakness, some lacking of self. But maybe that's just the way I'm hearing it. Maybe the oppressive specter of the Strong Black Woman/Black Superwoman haunts only me and not my sisters. Maybe their white female friends and acquaintances were not constantly saying to them, "You're the strongest person I know!" even as they stood there and crumbled. Maybe these women had not, in fact, internalized the notion that not only should Black women not expect to be loved, they should not even desire it.

Apparently, I had.

During this time I watched old reruns of the *Dick Cavett Show*. Cavett was an awkward, slow-witted and deeply unfunny interviewer (Lord, give me the career of a mediocre white man) but his show attracted extraordinary guests, including Lauren Bacall and Lena Horne. One night I watched Bacall discuss how she was punished, career-wise, for being human and refusing to try to live up to all the impossible fantasies America heaps upon the white female body and white female heart.

Another night I watched Horne discuss how she was punished, soul-wise, for being human, to refusing to live down to all those other American fantasies, the ones of Black women. "I was very icy for many years," she told Cavett. "I could not be at ease with you or many people, because of the ice society had put around my heart. When things that happened to me broke my heart I realized I wasn't my ice. I was very fragile, very human and a woman who had been this way for protection."

Both women impressed me. Only Lena Horne made me cry.

In the face of dehumanization, any expression of one's humanity is both resistance and reinforcement. In launching myself into online dating I admitted—to my friends, the world and most of all myself,—that, yes, I wanted to be loved, that I yearned for companionship and caretaking and connection. Instead of pretending to have it all together, I announced it was sometimes perilously close to falling apart. Like anybody else.

I wrote a profile and found a photo and posted them: Love Wanted.

It felt good.

II.

Seeing how many men desire you *as you are* is empowering.

Toni Morrison: "It was as though some mysterious all-knowing master had given each one a cloak of ugliness to wear, and they had each accepted it without question. The mast had said, "You are ugly people." They had looked

*about themselves and saw nothing to contradict the state-
ment; saw, in fact, support for it leaning at them from
every billboard, every movie, every glance. "Yes," they had
said. "You are right."*

In America, telling Black women what's wrong with
them is always good for a cheap laugh (DL Hughley), political
advancement (Clarence Thomas) or a bestselling book, movie
and bewildering-successful career (the execrable Steve Harvey).
In some (not all) Black churches the preaching of Proverbs 31
("Who can find a virtuous woman? for her price is far above
rubies . . . She seeketh wool, and flax, and worketh willingly
with her hands . . . she bringeth her food from afar. She riseth
also while it is yet night, and giveth meat to her household . . ."
etc). is an evergreen, a club used to clobber women into submissive, virginal behavior while they wait passively to be found
worthy of some man's love. The idea that Black women are
unworthy beggars at the table of love (and thus better fix themselves or die trying) grows like crabgrass out of the compacted,
grub-ridden lawn of white supremacy and misognynoir. It's
a big lawn; a lot of people wander on to it without thinking,
having absorbed myths about Black women—and especially
dark-skinned Black women—as Mammies (loud, fat, domes-
tically asexual) or Jezebels (hypersexual, animalistic, loud) or
Sapphires (aggressive, angry, loud).

Even the very narrative around online dating twists
against Black women. Data about user racial preferences from
OKCupid, one of the largest free dating websites, consistently
places Black women (and Asian men) at the bottom of the

desirability heap.[3] According to OKC, some 80 percent of non-Black men on the website apply a "penalty" to Black women, meaning they are less likely to either message them or respond to their messages than with white, Latino or Asian women. Even Black men, who generally tend to show no racial preference either way, tend to rate Black women slightly lower than Latino or Asian women. (Though not white women. Which is interesting).

This kind of thing can get a girl down, no matter how much she dusts herself in BlackGirlMagic. It is difficult not to notice how rarely Black women are celebrated as desirable and beautiful, even in movies and television shows hemmed by Black men. It is difficult not to notice that even when the love interests of Black male characters in movies and on hit television shows *are* Black women they are usually fair-skinned[4, 5] (*ER, This is Us, black-ish, Daredevil, Luke Cage, Atlanta,* Uhuru in the rebooted *Star Trek* movies, etc). It is difficult not to notice how many of one's fly and fabulous sister friends are unwillingly single, or how many of one's steady and serious brother friends (not to mention race men like Sidney Poitier, James Earl Jones, Donald Glover, Harry Belafonte, the list goes on and on . .). are partnered with/married to white women. The fact that Black men are twice as likely as Black women to marry someone of another race, a statistic that does not hold true for white, Asian or Hispanic men,[6] says nothing about any specific person or relationship. But it sure as hell says something about American society, and about the interplay between social structures and what we like to think of as individual agency.[7]

To be sure: plenty Black girls grow to adulthood un-nicked

by the knives of misogynoir. But many of us spend a lifetime bandaging the cuts. I grew up without a father, who, after my parents' divorce, largely absented himself from concern about our lives. My mother, herself under-loved and under-valued, focused her energies primarily on not letting us die: she didn't have a lot of time for building our self-esteem. I was the third of five children, middle girl and middle child. I thought myself weirdly tall, embarrassingly short-haired, depressingly fat. All of this would have been tempered had I had the good sense to be born closer to my mother's golden-brown skin color than my father's ebony tone but I did not. Thus, when the junior high boys in whom I was interested failed to return that interest, I was pretty sure I knew the reason: Not light enough, not long-haired enough, not skinny enough, i.e. not pretty at all. I never really wanted to be white, but there were days I would have taken being less Black.

Confirmation of this wish came from television, always on in our house. *The Love Boat* and *Fantasy Island* and *Starsky and Hutch* and *The Rockford Files* and *Mary Tyler Moore.* Of the few Black folks on television, most were men and most of them were laughable: JJ Evans, Fred Sanford, Rerun. What television made clear was that Black women, and especially dark-skinned Black women, were only visible in certain places, and when they were they were worthy of ridicule (Aunt Ester) or pity (a widowed Florida Evans) or, at best, jolly, maternal affection (Mabel King and Theresa Merritt on *What's Happening!* and *That's My Mama).* Never adoration. Never passion. Rarely love.

Who was worthy of these things? Farrah. Also, Barbara, Angie, Jaclyn. These women were pretty and that their prettiness extended, first and foremost, from their whiteness was without question.[8] By the time I reached high school the lack of interest from boys seemed to confirm my suspicion of un-desirability. To be sure, plenty of white girls grow up thinking themselves unattractive. Few, however, think themselves unattractive *because* of their whiteness. This is the difference.

The general lack of male interest continued in college, until eventually arrived a man who said, "I choose you." He was a good and decent man but that was mostly luck; I might have easily ended up with a charming sociopath (and later did). Instead I married this good and decent man and things were good for awhile and then fine for awhile and then not-so-fine and then really not fine at all. The marriage ended and when it did, I was fairly certain I'd reached the end of romantic love. I was forty-two, raising two children and living in Boston (that most progressive of faux-progressive towns), still tall, still Black and still believing, despite hard and conscious work, in my own unattractiveness. And the available data backed me up.

After forty, even if you live in a city, as I do, and work for a large institution and have many friends and attend many events and use public transportation and just generally refrain from living beneath a rock, even if you do all of that the number of age-appropriate, single, straight, interesting and interested men one meets in a given week is limited. The first man to ask me out in the non-digital world was a gray-haired drunk at a bar where my friend and I sat having dinner. The second was a lawyer-turned-convicted embezzler who'd converted to Buddhism on the inside, seen me on television, read my essay on depression and shown up at a reading worried about my mental health (and also interested in a date). These two invitations years apart. Combined with the drumming narrative, spawned by OKCupid's data dump and some women's personal experience, that online dating was not only unproductive but actively hostile to Black women, I almost gave up.[9]

Sister, I am telling you: don't believe the hype.

When I finally took the plunge into online dating the waters were indeed murky. Some men looked at my profile and declined to message me, or did not respond when I worked up the nerve to message them. Some men made clear in their profiles they did not find Black women attractive. Other men straight out told me I was not for them. In isolation these slings and arrows are wounding; in quantity they don't so much thicken the skin as make porous the ego, allowing passage straight through. Men rejected me for being too tall, too Black, too smart, too educated, too serious, too old, too laden with children, too far from their home. So many men rejected me, and so many more rejected some projection of me that I did not recognize, that taking it personally became impossible. It was either embrace the profound truth that rejection is not personal (neither, at bottom, is love, but that's another essay), that regardless of what another person says or does it is not about you, or stop getting out of bed. I kept getting out of bed.

Many men passed me over. But many, many more—and I mean hundreds of them, perhaps even a thousand over the years (I lost count)—pursued me. Tall men and short men, fit and not-so-fit, much older and much younger (!) smart men and not-so-bright, teachers, lawyers, bankers, telephone lineman, construction workers and snow-plow drivers, website designers and other vaguely techy guys, a movie producer, a bricklayer and at least one plastic surgeon (he was creepy). Black men and white men and Latino men and even Asian men, if you count Papua New Guinea and the Philippines, both of where I seemed, for some unknown reason, to be especially popular. The sheer volume (and, yes, variety) of offers, far beyond what any one woman could receive in one lifetime in the non-digital world, obliterated any hovering doubt about my desirability. (If white and Asian women receive magnitudes more attention online than I received, God bless them). Thus the specter of undesirability, which is really the ghost of unworthiness, was finally laid to rest.

For the first time in my life, the data worked for me.

III.

The choice is mine.

In the first, heady months of online dating I screened mostly for the negative. If a man messaged me and we chatted for awhile and he wasn't lewd or vulgar, blatantly unintelligent (uneducated was fine) or functionally illiterate, obtuse, racist or borderline misogynist, I said yes to meeting for coffee or a walk around some public spot. Even though my criteria eliminated probably 90 percent of the men who contacted me, I still met more men than I can remember and sat through more eye-glazing conversations than I care to recall.

Some of these men asked for a second date. Sometimes, out of loneliness or boredom or the unacknowledged belief that this was as good as it got, I said yes. At one point I said yes so often I ended up in a six-month relationship with a guy who made me wince every time he walked through the door.

"Why are you doing this if you're not excited?" asked a friend.

I spouted some nonsense about giving feelings time to grow but she knew that was bullshit. So did I.

Psychological research tells there is such a thing as too much choice. Having too many options, on the car lot or in television channels or in the cereal aisle, can not only paralyze the chooser but ultimately leave her less satisfied with whatever choice she makes.

But if too much choice can be unsettling, too little can constrain. How many women stay in relationships in which they are neglected or disrespected out of fear of being alone? How many women convince themselves, "It's better than nothing?" How many Black women?

Worse, what happens when disrespect crosses the line into violence? Women of all races, backgrounds and socioeconomic statuses experience domestic violence, but that experience is not the same. Poor women are more likely to be victims of domestic violence and their abuse is more likely to be severe, precisely because they lack the financial, emotional or psychological resources to escape.[10] In other words, they lack choice—or feel as if they do. "He consistently reminded me that no one else would ever love me like he did . . ."[11] is a common statement from abused women. The victim's belief in his or her essential unlovableness is one of the strongest weapons in the abuser's arsenal.

A few years ago I discovered that my mother had, in fact,

briefly dated after divorcing my father. She had one boyfriend, a man she declared the love of her life. But this man did not want the responsibility of raising five young children who were not his own, and so his choice was to move on. My mother too had a choice: she did not abandon us, as her mother had abandoned her. She made a choice but she didn't experience it that way, for reasons both personal and hegemonic. She made a choice but to her the choice felt like no choice at all. And so we the children did not feel chosen, while what she felt was mostly trapped.

It took awhile for me to stop saying yes to kind and decent men in whom I had no interest and for whom I felt nothing more than gratitude but after many an eye-glazing meeting eventually I did. The emails kept coming; my discernment increased and my requirements grew. If few men met those requirements, that was okay by me; I was happier at home alone. I began taking long breaks from dating, only rejoining the game when I had time and energy and sometimes leaving as quickly as I had come. If you know, really know, that food will be available tomorrow, you don't have to stuff yourself tonight.

I went into the online dating wilderness to find a man, but in the end what I found was myself. You saw that coming.

I also, as it turned out, found a man. We call that icing on the cake.

Becky and Me

"If there is any class of people who need to be lifted out of the their airy nothings and selfishness, it is the white women of America."

—Frances Ellen Harper

In the scene from *Roots* I most remember, Missy Anne informs Kizzy that she is to become her property.

Missy Anne, played by America's then sweetheart Sandy Duncan, is the teenaged niece of Dr. William Reynolds, enslaver of the captured African named Kunta Kinte and his daughter Kizzy, played by the great Leslie Uggams.

Missy Anne (the name itself is Black shorthand for a White woman, a forerunner of "Becky,")[1] and Kizzy have grown up together. Missy Anne has even secretly taught Kizzy to write and read. She is delighted at the prospect of becoming the legal owner of her friend. Kizzy is less so; among other things, she doesn't want to leave her family. But she knows enough not to voice her displeasure; she feints and feigns until Missy Anne demands an answer.

"Kizzy, don't you want to be my slave?" the white woman pouts. "Aren't you my friend?"

Years later, when I tried to make my daughter watch the

series in the vain hope it would mean as much to her as it had as it had to me, much of the writing seemed dated, the settings stagy, the acting overbroad. But this scene still sliced; even my daughter felt it. "Oh my God," she said. "Can you believe that?"

By then I could.

Don't you want to be my slave? Aren't you my friend?

To which Kizzy, smart enough to know she has no alternative, responds, "Of course I'm your friend, Missy Anne!"

And thus the lie begins.

•

B: There's always a risk in dealing with white women and I'd rather not deal with it. It's too complicated. At the end of the day you don't want to have to go home and be thinking about some slick racist shit she said.

•

James Baldwin, in a review of the painful 1959 movie version of *Porgy and Bess*, wrote, "We still live, alas, in a society mainly divided into Black and white. Black people still do not, by and large, tell white people the truth and white people still do not want to hear it." I suppose we will see.

Generally speaking, it's not that I dislike white women. Generally speaking it's that I do not trust them. Generally speaking, most Black women don't.[2]

That's a big statement, impossible to either prove or disprove. I make it based upon a lifetime of observation and study, and also a highly unscientific survey of friends and friends of friends, ranging in age from twenty to "well-over-sixty." Among the findings: This distrust—or, more precisely, this absence of trust—seems to hold true whether or not the Black woman has lived and worked mostly in predominately-white environments, whether or not she actually has any white women friends or whether or not she feels this absence as a loss. Most women expressed a kind of matter-of-fact awareness of the situation ("Nope, nope, noppity nope!" was one woman's response to the question of whether she trusted white women) but a few expressed surprise at the discovery.

It's a very interesting question. I never thought about it, but now that I do I can't think of a single white girlfriend. I don't think it's on purpose and I don't actually have a lot of friends but the few friends I have bonded from shared values and experiences that are common. Obviously trust is a big part of friendship.

It is important to note that every single Black woman to whom I spoke began with some version of the following: "Most of my friends are Black." This is a choice, not an exclusion, a positive statement of preference. Woman after woman says as much in some fashion and time after time I nod my head. *Girl, I understand.* This is also my preference, and I'm cool with it . . . but my sociological imagination wonders. I'm friends mostly with Black women because I prefer to be friends mostly with Black women because Black women can truly be my friends. Egg and chicken. All the white kids are sitting together in the lunchroom and so are all the Black children. Everybody prefers it this way. But why?

Most of the women I spoke to did count at least one

white woman among their inner circle. This woman is usually "woke"; she's been through "the ugly conversations—where we talk about complicated issues"; she "attempts to understand the struggle Black women face"; she "does not belittle my struggles nor discredit my movements." In some cases, rare and wonderful, she is not only woke but an "anti-racist conspirator, an ally in the most amazing ways," who "owns all of what it means to be a white person and a white woman in this fight."

Almost all of these women became the Black woman's friend during a formative period —high school, college, young adulthood. Many of the Black women had formed friendships of a kind with white women later in life, but these friendships went only so deep and rarely outlasted the circumstances of their formation:

M (a physician): After thinking, I have not maintained close female relationships with white women from work that lasted after leaving a particular practice.

B: I just remembered, I did have several white girlfriends in the Army. We were not as close as my Black girlfriends and we did not keep up after the Army like my other friends.

M: My relationship with white women has changed over the years because I have changed. I used to feel that you could be friends with everyone who was nice to you. I have since learned the difference between kind and nice. I have learned that people can be nice to your face and turn and say and do unkind things out of your presence. While I was in college it was easier to have white girlfriends because we were in class together. We had something in common but after college I soon realized that we are very different and have very different experiences.

A: I have a different relationship with the white friends I've made in college; I keep them at a distance. I take my time getting to know them and their views, and if they prove to be problematic then we're no longer friends but if they continually prove to be a true ally, then I value their friendship and hope that more people are like them in the world. My friendship isn't guaranteed like it's been in the past.

For my part, some of my best friends are white women. The first non-family member I ever lived with was a white woman and two of my bridesmaids and my rabbi friend and my lovely neighbors on either side. Two of the five people in the world I would call if the shit ever hit the fan are white women. Most of my co-workers and many of the people at my church. Just going by the attendees at my last birthday bash my social network is far more diverse than the average Black American (83 percent of social network also Black), Leaving in the dust any comparison to social network of the average white American (91 percent all-white).[3]

Interestingly, of my white friends, more are male than female. White men get a lot of bad press but I will say this much for them: you know where you stand. A white man, meeting a Black woman, generally wants to shoot her, fuck her, or crawl into her lap (combinations are naturally possible), and where one lands along this spectrum will be immediately discernible. Comments such as "I pulled you over because you were keeping pace with me and not speeding like everyone else,"[4] or "Oh, you're one of those arrogant Blacks!"[5] point in one direction. Comments such as, "Our family's maid practically raised me!" or "I love chocolate!"[6] point toward other paths.

But some white men stand outside of these positions; some white men have at least begun to free themselves from the shackles of history and hegemony and these men can meet you where you are. They'll probably want to be patted on the head for the effort, but a girl can't have everything. Either way with a white man, you know where you stand.

This is not the case with white women.

When I ask Black women why they have so few white female friends their answers range: "Too much trouble"; "They don't see me"; "Seems like something about us just sticks in their craw"—but seem to cluster around two major themes: power and invisibility.

Put simply, white women have power they will not share and to which they mostly will not admit, even when wielding it. Think about all the white women calling the police on Black women and men for capital crimes such as grilling near a lake, driving through a neighborhood, bumping a leg on an over-crowded plane. My uncle used to say, "White folks want to pee on your leg and call it rain!" Well, white women want to pee on your leg, have the police make you call it spring water and cry when you protest.

Moreover, white women simply don't see us. Not in the ways necessary for true sisterhood.

•

C: My distrust of white women at work has escalated. It wasn't something that I thought about a whole lot previously, but recently I've become aware of one who smiles in my face but whom I've

learned has done some serious backstabbing behind my, well, back . . .
And there are a couple others here whom a Black colleague of mine
has had a great deal of difficulty with . . .

POWER

White women sit at the right hand of power, leaning in, not down. There have been thirty-seven white female governors (and one each Latina and South Asian) but not a single Black female one. In fact, Black women represent just 2.7 percent of all female statewide elected officials. Seventeen of the twenty-one female US senators are white, as are the vast majority of female congressman. White women hold only 4.4 percent of CEO positions, but Black women hold a mere 0.2 percent. Every Equal Pay Day[7] white feminists decry the fact that women average 80 percent of a man's salary, but rarely mention that the figure applies mostly to white women: Latinas average 54 cents for every dollar, Black women average 68 cents, American Indian and Alaskan Native women make 58 cents. Far more concerning is the wealth gap: the wealth of white women swamps that of Black women—regardless of age, martial status or education level.[8]

White women are still far more likely than Black women to hold at least a bachelor's degree[9] (Asian women swamp everyone), be in the labor force[10] or own a business (or acquire the capital to fund a start-up) or be among the full-time faculty at a degree-granting institution.[11] In other words, even doing "the right things" doesn't help Black women a shred as much as it helps white women.

Yet rarely do white feminists take up the greater cause of Black female inequity. White women are among the most vocal and vociferous opponents of affirmative action, despite being equal, if not greater, beneficiaries.[12, 13]

White feminist heroes like Sheryl Sandberg come late to the acknowledgement of intersectionality, if they come at all: In her manifesto *Lean In*, Sandberg admits the privileges afforded her by class and education but sidesteps the privileges of whiteness while encouraging women to "lean in." The first comprehensive report on women in the business world by her organization did not even bother to break out data on women of color—data which really sucks.[14]

This is what Black women know: when push comes to shove, white women choose race over gender: Every. Single. Time. The election of Donald Trump with 54 (!) percent of the white female vote (but just 6 percent of Black women) is just one damaging (and damning) example; there are many more. Recall how slow white feminists were come to come to Michelle Obama's aid when she was being savaged during the 2008 campaign,[15] how quick they were later to jump on her for not being "feminist" enough,[16] how absent are their voices when Black women are being shot and beaten by cops?

Going further back, remember how the first women's rights movement in the United States emerged from the campaign to abolish slavery—but later split over the question of race?[17] Free Black women such as Frances Harper, Maria Stewart and Sojourner Truth worked alongside white women such as Angelina and Sarah Grimke and Elizabeth Cady Stanton to end the peculiar institution, but parted ways over the question of who should get the vote first: Black men or white women. Harper, the most prominent Black woman writer, speaker and abolitionist of her time, passionately supported the call for Black women's rights. But she believed that if a choice had to be made—and it seemed it did—then Black men had the more urgent need for federal protection. Harper cited the 1857 Dred Scott decision, which found that "men of my race had no rights which the white man was bound to respect."[18] To this view Stanton vehemently objected, arguing against enfranchising "Sambo" and "ignorant negroes and foreigners"[19] before white women. Both Stanton and Susan B. Anthony opposed the fifteenth amendment.

Then there was the Women's March.

From the sidelines (and definitely side-eyeing) I watched it begin. The day after Trump won the presidency of the United States, Teresa Shook, a white woman, created a Facebook event calling for a "Million Woman March." By the next morning I'd been tagged a dozen times by white colleagues and friends. My first thought was, "Is this supposed to be a continuation of the one in Philly?" Meaning the march and gathering which brought an estimated 750,000 Black women to Philadelphia in 1997, two years after the Million Man March in DC. But no: it turned out that Shook had never heard of that historic event.[20] So that didn't bode well.

The Internet being the Internet, Shook was quickly given a history lesson. The march leadership was expanded to include such veteran organizers as Linda Sarsour, Carmen Perez, and Tamika Mallory, all women of color. Icons like Maxine Waters and woke famous people like Janelle Monae were invited to speak and perform. Still, most of my Black women friends were like, "Meh."

But the white women were all abuzz! Many of my white colleagues asked if I was going. A white woman I did not know approached me in the CVS to inquire. She, like the others, was super excited: for many of them, it was their first march. They'd been busy, I suppose, when we marched when Trayvon Martin was killed and when Michael Brown was killed and when Tamir Rice was killed and when their killers got off. But they were showing up now. For what? "For women!"

At a dinner party a white woman told me she had purchased a facemask and armed herself with jugs of milk. I blinked at her.

"Seriously? Why?"

"In case the police attack us!"

"When was the last time you saw police attack a group of white women?" I asked. She fumbled through a reply but we both knew it was ridiculous: had she really thought the possibility of danger existed she would not have been leaving her house.

"They won't attack *white* women," I told her. "They'll probably hand out daisies."

"Bottles of waters," said another Black woman friend.

"Swag," I added.

The night of the march I met a lovely, middle-aged white woman and her white husband from a white town in white central Massachusetts (I was at a white party, one of three colored folk in the room). She and her neighbor and their daughters had attended the Sister march in Boston and she was still glowing from the experience: how exhilarating it was. How powerful and connected she felt. What fun.

Did she want to talk about police brutality against Black people? About systemic racism in the justice system? About segregation in schools? "I'm not very political," she said.

I nodded. "That must be nice."

This kind of pick-and-choose righteousness is the reason Black women roll their eyes at pom-pom white feminists like Patricia Arquette, who blithely demand that "All the women in America and all the men that love women, and all the gay people, and all the people of color that we've all fought for fight for us now." (Setting aside the question of when, precisely, Patricia Arquette fought for people of color, who does she mean by "us?"

Likewise for Taylor Swift, who responded to Nicki Minaj's request for solidarity in calling out the sidelining of Black female artists, with superficial declarations of feminism ("It's not like you to pit women against one another") and facile declarations of love ("I've done nothing but love and support you).[21]

"I love u just as much," tweeted Minaj. "*But u should speak on this.*"

Swift: "If I win, please come up with me!! You're invited to any stage I'm ever on."

Don't you want to be my slave? Aren't you my friend?

That white women do not want to relinquish their spot on the second rung is to be expected. "Power concedes nothing without a demand," wrote Frederick Douglass. "Never has, never will." It's the pretense that's maddening.

Every fall I teach a survey class in African-American literature, an undertaking I consider one of the chief honors of my life. One of my favorite books to teach in this class is Harriet Jacob's seminal slave narrative, *Incidents in the Life of a Slave Girl.* Authenticated as the first, book-length slave narrative authored by a woman, *Incidents* is a powerful and compelling examination of slavery's impact on Black women and the Black family. After working their way through Olaudah Equiano's dense but trailblazing slave narrative and Frederick Douglass' brilliant, iconic one, the students are eager to hear a woman's perspective. Jacobs does not let them down.

"Slavery is terrible for men, but it is far more terrible for women," she writes in the narrative's most famous line. The students nod. They're with Jacobs as she details the physical, psychological and sexual terrorism of slavery. They're with her as she asserts the resilience and importance of Black kinship. They're definitely with her as she critiques the hypocritical Christianity of the south.

But when Jacobs gets around to criticizing white women—both Southern white women who turn a blind eye to their husband's rape and debasement of enslaved women *and* Northern white women who, enraptured by the romantic myth of the wealthy southern gentleman, also turn a blind eye—some students begin to balk. Without fail at least one young white woman will raise her hand, eyes determined, chin quivering:

"Yes, but all women were property back then."[22] Or "Gender discrimination has always been a bigger problem than racism." Or "Well, white women didn't have it much better than slaves." Which is simply untrue.[23]

I find these moments revealing,[24] the student's face both

intense and needy as she mounts her defense of white women past. If there is a Black woman student in the class (there isn't always) I watch her face as her classmate speaks, and I watch both faces to see who sees who. I lay out some facts about the rights and restrictions upon white women in pre-Civil War America and I see the resistance. I think: if this student, who is young but neither thoughtless nor ill-informed, insists on believing that white women in 1850 were as oppressed as enslaved people, if she cannot and will not acknowledge the power differentials that existed within a system of legal, racialized slavery, how can she grapple honestly with the power imbalances of today? And if she won't, how can she and her Black classmate possibly be friends?

Audre Lord asked, "If white American feminist theory need not deal with the differences between us, and the resulting difference in our oppressions, then how do you deal with the fact that the women who clean your houses and tend your children while you attend conferences on feminist theory are, for the most part, poor women and women of Color? What is the theory behind racist feminism?"

James Baldwin put it even more bluntly: "One can be, indeed one must strive to become, tough and philosophical concerning destruction and death, for this is what most of mankind has been best at since we have heard of man. (But remember: *most* of mankind is not *all* of mankind). But it is not permissible that the authors of devastation should also be innocent. It is the innocence which constitutes the crime."

•

A: The relationship between white women and Black women has an overall competitive nature that I feel is partially one-sided. White women copy Black women often and then feel the need to rebrand what they copied as their own.

M: In general, it feels like competitiveness. For exactly what I am not sure. Men? Education? Careers? Money? Status?

C: I think that we are particularly threatening to them, partly because most of us are so bad—smart, attractive, and resilient, and I think they cannot stand it . . . But it's also puzzling because they have all the cards, so to speak. They are the right hand of white men, and therefore have all the power, so why go after us? Is it just sadism?

•

A woman I know—capable, intelligent, and, incidentally, deeply-Christian and kind—was awarded a $10.9 million verdict for discriminatory treatment in her position in the city of Boston's Treasury Department.[25] The prime culprit? A white woman, the First Assistant-Collector Treasurer, who, the jury found, not only engaged in a pattern of discrimination against my friend and other Black employees but retaliated when my friend filed a complaint, pressuring her immediate supervisor to give her a negative performance review (which he refused to do), sneakily hiding a job posting so she could not apply, and disciplining her for the first time in her long career, labeling her "aloof, non-deferential, and uppity."

Don't you want to be my slave? Aren't you my friend?

Is this sadism? Plain old-fashioned American racism? Some sparkly, pink combination? Decades and lifetimes ago

I worked as a reporter for *The New York Times*. The Great, Gray Lady was in the middle of a Manhattan Spring, a brief and fleeting easing of the newsroom's relentless Whiteness.[26] They'd gone on a hiring spree. At a newsroom meeting a Black male reporter who had recently returned from abroad turned to me.

"Don't take this wrong way, but have you noticed that every single Black or Latino woman they're hired over the past year, including yourself, is hot?"

As a matter of fact, I had. It was glaringly obvious to anyone that every single Black or brown woman hired in the newsroom rush (most of whom later left in disenchantment) was not only capable, talented, well-educated, accomplished and ambitious, they were also above average in societally-accepted standards of attractiveness. Which was not universally the case among the white female reporters—and sure as hell was not the case among white men.

My point is not that all Black girls are magic. The world is full of mediocre Black women; they just don't tend to do very well. My point is that just to make it to the *New York Times*, a Black woman had (has) to be not only good but extraordinary, even in ways that should not count. Simply to enter the spaces where white women are likely to come into contact with us Black women have to be superlative in ways that white women do not. If this makes white women feel competitive and even threatened, I can understand. But don't take that shit out on us—and when you do, don't pretend that you're not. Also don't deny that in most arenas, in education, income, wealth and status, white women still hold the winning hand.

INVISIBILITY

V: I feel white women approach me in one of two ways: either they don't see me or they are sizing me up.

In 2012 the actress Viola Davis and several other Oscar nominees conducted a joint interview with a journalist. Davis expounded upon the difficulty of being a Black actress in Hollywood, especially a dark-skinned one: "I'm a forty-six-year-old Black woman who really doesn't look like Halle Berry, and Halle Berry is having a hard time—"

The white actress Charlize Theron cut her off: "I'm going to have to stop you there for a second 'cause that's bullshit."

"Why, you think I look like Halle Berry?"

"No. You have to stop saying that because you are hot as shit. You look amazing," Theron declared.

Which is not remotely the point. Theron interpreted a criticism of deeply-racialized beauty standards in Hollywood as a feeble cry of low self-esteem. She sat right in front of a Black woman trying to explain her experience—and cut her off, leaping in to save Davis with useless cheerleading.

Did she mean well? No doubt. White women lounge all along our road to hell, meaning well. Theron has been cast in thirty-five major movies, with an adjusted total gross of more than $2 billion. Davis has been cast in twenty-five movies with an adjusted total gross of $1.4 billion. Theron has been the face of high-profile ad campaigns for glamorous luxury brands such as Christian Dior. Davis has not. Davis has an estimated net worth of $3 million. Theron's is $110 million. *You're pretty too.*

M: It is difficult to explain. But I don't entirely feel comfortable letting my guard down completely. In the past, I had white girl-friends I thought we were really close only to learn I was some sort of token or charity case. It made me very skeptical of other offers of friendship from other white women. I am friends with them but I keep a certain distance.

•

V: In general their assumption is whatever they give us we're going to take.

Aristotle defined friendship as "reciprocated goodwill." What distinguishes friendships, he wrote, is the *source* of this goodwill.

In friendships of pleasure or utility the bond extends from the benefits we receive from the relationship: either pleasure or usefulness. By contrast, in friendships of virtue, the bond extends simply from the other person—we love our friend simply because she is who she is. Aristotle considered nothing wrong with the first two types of friendship; even friendships of utility do not necessarily involve exploitation—tennis buddies and work friends are mutually beneficial, and anyone who has been a mother knows about the transient existence of "mommy" friends.

But Aristotle considered friendships of virtue—in which each person values the person for her own sake and supplies goodwill toward that person, even above her own interests, for no other reason than because of who the friend is—the only perfect form of friendship. Pleasure and usefulness change or fade—you change jobs or stop playing tennis or your children grow up and the friendship fades away. Friendships based on personhood endure as long as the person endures. People grow (well, some people . . .). but they rarely really change—for better or for worse.

Friendships of virtue are only possible among "good people similar in virtue," Aristotle wrote, because only good people are capable of loving others for their own sake and of placing that person's wellbeing above her own. The catch here is that to love someone simply because of who she is, one must first actually *see* that person for who she really is. Not a stereotype or a fantasy, neither a charity case nor an abstract threat. Just a human being.

This is where, between Black women and White women, things get hard.

C: The thing is, a lot of times I'm all about the sisterhood. There's always a tiny little piece of me that says maybe she's gonna be okay. But then I see them not embracing that sisterhood in the same way. Nine out of ten times they're not gonna embrace that and I'm gonna be left holding the bag.

At the core of love is vulnerability; so, too, friendship. To be vulnerable is to be human and to be human is to be vulnerable, whether we like it or not. But the brutal truth is that many white women, like much of white America in general, do not consider Black women vulnerable, which means they do not consider us to be fully human. To confirm this takes only a passing glance at pop cultural depictions of Black women, at the ugly, debasing vitriol directed at Michelle Obama, at the ways in which Black mothers mourning for their slain sons at the hands of police officers are dismissed and demeaned.

Friendship is not possible between a human being and one who doubts her humanity—whether that doubt is framed in terms of the Angry Black Woman or, just as damagingly, the Black Superwoman.

At the last high school reunion I bothered to attend I had a conversation with a classmate, a woman I had known but not well. She began the ritual remembrance of intimidating teachers and painful heartbreaks, blistering self-consciousness and bewildering adolescence, intensified by being at one of the nation's top boarding schools. I said something along the lines of, "Yeah, we were all pretty much scared shitless," and she said, "Not you! You were always so strong and confident!"

This would be laughable if it weren't also revealing and sad. I was a poor Black girl who had been plucked from the bunch at my Memphis public school and shipped unwilling and terrified off to New Hampshire to diversify the prep school, or at least put a good front. I was overwhelmed, terrified and alone.

But this chick saw me as "strong and confident." Which would be forgivable except for the fact that twenty-five years later, when I tried to correct her impression, she still refused to hear.

I wrote a piece about how Black women are not allowed to be vulnerable. And this white female classmate wrote me three pages of notes telling me I didn't understand feminism and that she guessed Black women needed other avenues of thought but that really we should just focus on the universal sisterhood and how I need to redefine womanist. I'm like: are you Alice Walker? How are you going to tell me what it means to be a womanist!? Then she's trying to friend me on Facebook and I'm like: we are not friends.

And of course many Black women respond to this hegemonic instruction, which begins almost at birth, by either tamping down or simply masking vulnerability. We don't show it because white America can't see it. White America can't see it because we don't show. Egg and chicken, chicken and egg.

"For women, the need and desire to nurture each other is not pathological but redemptive," wrote Lorde, "and it is within that knowledge that our real power is rediscovered."

The key words here are "each other"—white women must not only expect nurturing but must nurture in return.

•

I keep going back to that scene, trying to figure out why it resonates. Two women sit on the earth facing one another; between them, invisible but potent, lies both their own interpersonal history and the history of the society in which they live. Missy Anne, who blinks innocence but who knows enough about the prevailing power structure to know on which side she stands ("Black people are slaves and white people own them. That's just the way it is") promises to always protect Kizzy. Because they are friends.

But when Kizzy's young love Noah is caught trying to escape with a pass forged by Kizzy, Waller sells her off as punishment. In a brutal, heartbreaking scene Kizzy is dragged away screaming and crying while her distraught parents beg for mercy.

"You think that's the moment when your best friend is going to say, "No! You can't sell her. That's my friend!" explained the actress and singer Leslie Uggams, who played Kizzy. 'And Missy Anne does nothing, because Missy Anne is ticked off that she would dare write a note for somebody. 'You're supposed to be *my* friend.'"

Don't you want to be my slave?

"That's heartbreaking [for Kizzy.] What your mother has been trying to tell you [has become apparent.] 'You may play together, but she is not your friend."

Audre Lorde: "As women, we have been taught either to ignore our differences, or to view them as causes for separation and suspicion rather than as forces for change. Without community there is no liberation, only the most vulnerable and temporary armistice between an individual and her oppression. But community must not mean a shedding of our differences, nor the pathetic pretense that these differences do not exist."

In the book *Roots* Kizzy and Missy Anne never meet again. But in the miniseries they meet many years later, when both are very old. It's been a brutal life for Kizzy—rape heartbreak, abandonment—though she has managed to raise a family and pass on her father's Mandinka ways. Missy Anne travels past the planation where Kizzy is still enslaved and stops to ask for a cup of water. Kizzy recognizes Missy Anne, and states her own name.

"I'm sorry but I don't recollect ever knowing a darkie named Kizzy," Missy Anne replies.

Leslie Uggams: "You did all this to me now you still are not acknowledging me? You don't recognize me? I think there was a glimmer of hope in Kizzy. She was thinking that maybe . . ." Uggams shakes her head. "Nothing. So she says, You're nothing to me either.' And she spits in the cup."

The look on Kizzy's face as Duncan drinks and the jaunty music that plays beneath the scene casts the moment as one of triumph, but I don't know: the scales still seem unbalanced to me.

Don't you want to be my slave?
No. Nor anything resembling.
Aren't you my friend?
Well, I guess that depends.

Eshu Finds Work

In July, as Eshu is chasing me down, I stumble across a newspaper article about a group of men in London who like to dress and live like dogs. These men, these members of the "pup community," spend their time dozing on the floor and leaping around with squeaky toys. They roll in the dirt. They nuzzle their human handlers.

The article makes it clear these men seek only acceptance as they are, which I am certainly willing to grant. Still, I can't help but think of a phrase from my childhood, a phrase about which I am ambivalent but which I cannot completely disavow: *Now that is some white folks' mess.*

"White folks' mess" was a phrase used often by the adults in my Black, southern family—especially the women—a phrase by which a whole host of bewildering behaviors and events could be explained: Pet Rocks and deviant sexual practices, backwoods camping and fifty dollars for a pair of ripped jeans. Kissing your dog. Serial killers. *Happy Days* and Ronald Reagan and Barry Manilow.

And mental illness. Mental illness, mental disorder of any possible stripe, was definitely white folks' mess. White people had nervous breakdowns; Black folks just got tired of shit. White people had anxiety, Black folks had *nerves*. Black folks got the blues sometimes, but only white people got clinically depressed. White people listened to Prozac. Black folks listened to their mother, their pastor, and God.

All of which explains why, although I don't precisely remember at what age I came to understand as depression the unpredictable trickster threatening to submerge me, it's not hard for me to guess the time period. It would not be while I still lived at home under the sole influence of my mother, a tough and (secretly) wounded bird. It would have to be after I was sent, protesting and frightened and in the name of diversity, from Memphis to a predominately rich, predominately New England and very, very white boarding school at the age of fifteen.

Confirmation arrives in the form of my old journal:

May 17, 1981: And instead of doing homework I'm writing here. I feel like I'm teetering on the edge of that old familiar feeling of depression and I need something to pull me back. I don't know what.

Depression: I actually used the word here, just a few days past my birthday.

I had just turned seventeen.

•

A few days after reading about the "pup community," I open a file on my computer and begin writing up drafts of suicide notes.

This is not so much the start of any coherent plan as it is a means of confronting head-on the tricky spirit that has been loping around the past few weeks, sharpening its claws, readying its cruel and damaging pranks. It occurs to me that, for a writer, a suicide note is no minor thing: one's last literary production, one's final words to the world. Talk about pressure. What do you say that makes sense that won't embarrass you in your biography? What do you say even if you know no one will ever write a biography of you?

I decide to do a little research. Famous writers and their suicide notes. I begin, predictably, with Papa:

July 2, 1961. Ernest Hemingway climbs from bed at his house in the Sawtooth Mountains early in the morning, walks to the storage room where his beloved firearms are kept, takes out a double-barreled shotgun, and shoots himself.

I hate guns but Hemingway kept a lot of them. Firearms are, by far, the most common method of suicide: 55 percent of people who take their own lives do so by firearm, according to data from the Centers for Disease Control. Nearly two-thirds of the gun-related deaths in the United States each year are suicides, meaning the majority of people who die by gun in America do so at their own hand. Gun suicides are especially prevalent among men.

Hemingway, that man among men, did not leave a note. In *Death in the Afternoon*, however, he wrote this: "There is no lonelier man in death, except the suicide, than that man who has lived many years with a good wife and then outlived her. If two people love each other there can be no happy end to it."

Perhaps Hemingway killed himself because he feared a decline of his vaunted masculinity, or the loss of his prodigious writing skills. Perhaps he feared losing Mary, who lay sleeping upstairs when he pulled the trigger and presumably heard the shot. Perhaps he was just tired, and wanted to go out on his own terms.

Nobody really knows, though plenty of people have speculated. That's what happens when you don't leave a suicide note: people can make up any shit they want.

•

In 2016, an estimated 16.2 million adults (6.7 percent of the adult population) experienced at least one major depressive episode, according to the National Institute of Mental Health. A major depressive episode is defined as a period of two weeks or longer during which a person experiences depression, loss of interest or pleasure in everyday life, *and* at least four other symptoms that reflect a change in functioning: sleeplessness or excessive sleeping, loss of appetite, or problems with energy, concentration or self-image. (An important note: the NIMH did not make exclusions for depression caused by bereavement, substance abuse, or medical illness).

Women are 70 percent more likely than men to experience depression in their lifetime, says the CDC. On the bright side, depression among women improves after age sixty, which is not true of men.

Not surprisingly, people living below the poverty level are more than twice as likely to experience depression as those living at or above the poverty line. The National Survey of American Life finds that African Americans are less likely than whites to experience depression (lasting over two weeks) over their lifetimes. But the US Health and Human Services Office of Minority Health finds that adult African Americans are 20 percent *more* likely than whites to report serious psychological distress at any given time.

How to make sense of the discrepancy? Perhaps Black Americans get depressed more often than their white counterparts but bounce back in less than two weeks. There is some evidence for this—a study by the University of Michigan found the link between depression and hopelessness was stronger among white Americans than Black Americans. Or maybe Black Americans are simply less likely to admit being depressed. There is evidence too for this theory: Black Americans are half as likely as their white counterparts to access mental health services. An estimated 92 percent of African-American men with depression do not seek help, according to the CDC. Which makes it reasonable to consider that the statistics may be off.

Here's one more statistic from the CDC: the portion of people with depression who will commit suicide is 15 percent.

All of this is of probing, compelling interest to the observer part of me. To observe a thing is to wonder, to wonder is to contemplate, to contemplate is to determine, to determine is to understand. Not that understanding offers a solution or an escape.

The other part of me, the experiencing part, I struggle to name. "Depression," yes, but how pedestrian and limited that word is. The "monster" I know is too melodramatic and un-ambivalent for such a name. (What did Joan Didion write in *Slouching Towards Bethlehem*? "I can't get that monster out of my mind.")

I try "spirit," then "satyr," then "trickster," but none of those is right. Then it comes to me: Eshu. The trickster god of the Yoruba people. Sly, disruptive, unpredictable, and randomly either helpful or cruel, he serves as a messenger between the people and their gods. Eshu.

The other part of me, the observer who stands outside Eshu and watches him tricking me down into the depths, is easy to name. She's the Writer. I've known her all along.

•

Usually the misery is worse in winter. I am a southern girl, not born for long, dark days of snow and cold. The brief New England summer is usually a blessing, the sun and heat (I never use an air conditioner) like a natural antidepressant buoying me up.

But the year of our Lord 2015 brings reversal. The Boston winter is so off-the-charts unbearable that even the embrace-the-cold types are miserable. And I am strangely okay.

Then comes spring and then summer, blessed summer, and my spirits plunge. May into June, June into sweet, hot July. There are no reasons for my sadness: all is well, if not perfect, in my life. I am blessed with many gifts. Yet the days begin in quicksand and grow heavier. I cry consistently. I read the news and see only ugliness: police brutality and racial injustice, war and rampant greediness, babies dying in Chicago and babies washed up on a European beach. A friend has an eleven-year-old son battling cancer and the updates on Facebook wrench my heart. Another friend struggles with financial ruin and a third leaks loneliness. The whole world seems selfish and irredeemably cruel and I feel alone in it: unprotected, un-chosen, unloved.

For my children only I get up off the couch and try the things people who have never been depressed so blithely recommend. I exercise and get some sun, take the dog for long, rambling walks. I focus on others, on my kids and my volunteer work. I go to church and count my blessings and practice gratitude. I try 5HTP, a so-called natural antidepressant. I try saying, lightly, of my yawning, aching loneliness, "Oh well!"

I try to meditate. Psychological research, including a 2014 *JAMA Internal Medicine* analysis of forty-seven studies, suggests that meditation and mindfulness-based cognitive therapy can be moderately effective in treating depression and perhaps more so at preventing relapse. Then again, psychological research (a 2015 meta-analysis published in the journal *Science*) suggests that 60 percent of psychological research is, essentially, crap.

Some of these things work temporarily, like licking your lips when they are chapped. Soon enough the relief evaporates. Soon enough the stinging returns.

Near the bottom of the tumble I begin calling on people for help. This is almost always a mistake. One has to be very careful who one talks to in the midst of a depressive episode; not everyone is your friend, not even your friends. People want to be helpful, but what they think of as help is less like tossing a rope to a drowning person and more like tossing an anvil.

What could possibly be the matter? You're fine.

It's always darkest . . . God never closes a door . . . smile and the world smiles . . . Come on! You're a strong Black woman!

This kind of help stems partly from good intentions but also from a pervasive societal belief that depression is really a kind of moral failure: a bad attitude, a shortage of will. (Percentage of people who think depression is a personal weakness according to the US Department of Health and Human Services: 54. Percent of Black people who think so: 65). In the United States of America, land of the eternally young and the eternally cheerful, complexity of feeling is suspect. Anyone disinclined toward the warm bath of relentless happiness risks being branded "negative." Once, on a date, a man I had just met asked me if I believed I would find my soul mate. I refrained from saying I didn't believe in soul mates (or that research shows people who believe in soul mates are less satisfied in their relationships) and said only that while I certainly hoped to find a partner someday, there was no guarantee I would.

He looked at me as if I'd pulled a puppy from my purse and drowned it in my water glass.

"With an attitude like that, I fear for your future!" he cawed. Exact words.

The deep American suspicion of melancholy and its contents is connected to the deep American suspicion of intellect, of complexity of thought and perspective, of wakefulness. Every institution in our culture, every Hollywood movie and major league game, every history lesson and Labor Day sale and political stump colludes to keep the dreamer dreaming, to tuck in the blanket and pat the heads. By default, depressives stand outside of this magical circle, observing. By necessity, they must be bullied back in.

I was probably forty years old before it occurred to me that not everyone felt things as deeply as I apparently do, that not everyone tumbled into canyons once or twice a month. I always just assumed other folks were better at leaping out.

That people should experience physical pain differently is pretty well accepted. Physicians and scientists speak of "pain tolerance" (the maximum level of pain a person is able to tolerate) and "pain thresholds" (the point at which pain begins to be felt) and how these differ in women and men. We understand that physical pain is not only a biochemical/neurological experience but also an emotional one; stick ten different people with a pin and they will experience the pain of that prick in ten different ways. Redheads are more sensitive to pain than others, and right-handed people can tolerate more pain in their right hands than in their left. When my daughter had surgery the PACU nurses kept asking her to rate her pain from one to ten. "Your five might be my eight, but it doesn't matter," they said. "It's how it feels to you that counts."

The last time I had blood drawn the young woman in the cubicle next to me was so panicky at the thought of the needle piercing her skin she burst into tears. They were still calming her down when I left.

Me, I have no problem with needles. I shrug off headaches, managed a second-degree burn with one dose of Tylenol, gave birth to both my kids without epidurals. Maybe that means I'm tougher than people who scream at cuts or moan at toothaches or demand relief from the agonies of labor. Or maybe that shit just didn't hurt me as much.

•

One in ten Americans now takes a daily antidepressant medication. Among women in their forties and fifties the number is one in four. The percentage has skyrocketed since the late 1980s and climbs more every day. Pretty much everyone except the makers of Wellbutrin and Paxil (etc). believes that this is far more than necessary, that physicians have over-diagnosed depression on a massive scale. *The Emperor's New Drugs: Exploding the Anti-Depressant Myth*, a 2009 book by Irving Kirsch, expanded on his research that found antidepressants were no more effective than placebo in treating all but the most severe cases of depression. But a new statistical analysis of the data in 2012, led by a researcher at Yale and using a statistical technique known as growth-mixture modeling, found that three-quarters of patients actually did better on medication than placebo—while one-quarter were actually made worse.

Regardless of and despite the overprescribing, and the confusion around efficacy, most mental health professionals agree that many people who meet the requirements for major depression suffer without treatment. This is especially true among African Americans and Latinos, who access mental healthcare services at far lower rates than their white counterparts. Our white counterparts.

Eshu visited sporadically but persistently from the time I wrote that journal entry at age seventeen. In college I sent him packing with panic over finances and crushes on boys and Saturday nights of rum, and still wrote stuff like this: "I'm scared I'll find there really is no meaning behind it all. Wouldn't that be funny, a joke on all us aspiring ambitious intellectuals? What if I struggle and fight and finally make it and go home one night to my luxury apartment and sit in the dark with Simon and Garfunkel on my thousand dollar stereo and cry because it doesn't really matter any damn way?" Ah, youth. (My Bose cost $150).

Out of college and working I tried once or twice seeing a therapist. These were either kindly old white women in rocking chairs who had not a clue where I was coming from or glossy young white women in stirrup pants and glinting diamond rings who had even less of a clue. I rarely got past session one.

I remember once lying on the floor of an apartment overlooking Broadway and 51st Street, an apartment owned by the *New York Times* and provided to me for free. I was twenty-seven or twenty-eight, newly married, newly hired by the best newspaper in the land, healthy, competent, and free, and yet I lay on that floor from sundown until past midnight, sobbing, pressed down, unable to move.

The one time during all those years I even considered antidepressants was during the fall of 2001. My husband and I had just moved to Boston and I found myself in a strange, unfriendly city with a toddler and a newborn and no community or family of my own. I struggled.

Worried more about my children, who were both at home all day alone with me, than myself, I finally saw my doctor, who casually prescribed some drug. I don't remember which antidepressant it was because after the first few doses I gave it up. I feared the drugs were numbing my emotions, stealing my ability to write. Whether this was true or imagined (most physicians believe it takes two to six weeks for antidepressants to have an affect) mattered not. Writing was the very thing that had saved my life all those years: if writing went, I might well die. I stopped taking the drugs, muscled my way through that particular episode.

Muscling one's way through depression is definitely an option. As long as one's muscles hold out.

•

March 28, 1941. Virginia Woolf walks out of her house in Sussex and into the River Ouse, her pockets loaded with stones. She leaves a letter for her devoted husband Leonard:

Dearest, I feel certain that I am going mad again. I feel we can't go through another of those terrible times. And I shan't recover this time. I begin to hear voices, and I can't concentrate. So I am doing what seems the best thing to do. You have given me the greatest possible happiness. You have been in every way all that anyone could be. I don't think two people could have been happier 'til this terrible disease came. I can't fight any longer. I know that I am spoiling your life, that without me you could work. And you will I know. You see I can't even write this properly. I can't read. What I want to say is I owe all the happiness of my life to you. You have been entirely patient with me and incredibly good. I want to say that—everybody knows it. If anybody could have saved me it would have been you. Everything has gone from me but the certainty of your goodness. I can't go on spoiling your life any longer. I don't think two people could have been happier than we have been.

•

It's late July and I stand in my kitchen, staring at the pile of dishes in the drainer and the crappy counters that won't get clean no matter how hard I scrub. It's Saturday afternoon, the children off with their father. The fact that I have managed, with much hard work, to help keep those relationships intact feels like the one success in a life dotted with failure. Which is ridiculous, I know. I know. And yet . . . I stand in the kitchen with my arms crossed tight, holding myself and considering.

There are two doorways, one to the hallway, the other to the dining room; they'd need to be covered up somehow, to keep the gas from spilling all over the house. I open my oven door and peek inside, searching for the pilot light. Do ovens even have pilot lights anymore? Has some enterprising spirit taken away that course? I can't find one but I do notice the oven is filthy. I should clean it.

I call a friend.

I'm really struggling here.

Oh, you're fine.

No, I'm not.

Yes, you are. You're fine. You're beautiful and smart and talented—what could be the problem? You're a little lonely and sad but you're fine.

Every day ten people in the United States accidentally drown. The vast majority of these deaths take place in spas and pools, and in many cases, especially with children, other people are present. They stand right there, right within reach, close enough to save the drowning person. If they would only turn around.

But drowning doesn't look the way it does in the movies. Drowning victims don't thrash and scream for help. They go down silently, their primal brain focused intently on what is happening. And so the people around them pay no mind.

You're fine.

My friend tells me I'm fine and I thank her and hang up and look at the draft suicide notes I have stored on my computer:

I've said enough. (Pithy and succinct).

I've said enough. No one listened anyway. (Melodramatic and self-pitying).

Everybody forgets that Icarus also flew. (Stole this from a wonderful poem. But it fits).

I told y'all I was tired.

The last one is my favorite. Terrible, I know, but reading it makes me laugh.

•

Not all writers are tortured geniuses. I know many stable writers, level-headed and content, writers who don't drink or take drugs or require antidepressants, writers who use, without irony, words like "optimist."

Still, there's no denying some subtle connection between creativity and mental anguish. Several studies have confirmed the link (Andresen, 1987; Jamison, 1989; Ludwig, 1995) even if they fail to explain it. The largest study to date to examine the connection was conducted by researchers at the Karolinska

Institute in Sweden. That study found that creative types, writers in particular, were overrepresented among people with schizophrenia, depression, bipolar disorder, anxiety syndrome, and substance abuse problems. Writers were also almost twice as likely to commit suicide as the general population.

The question, of course, is why? What's the chicken and what's the egg in this riddle? Does who we are determine what we become, or does what we become shape who we are? Are people with a certain way of looking at the world—a way that develops or engenders or supports melancholy, depression, despair—more likely to become writers? Or does being a writer and thus obligated to stare straight at the reality of what it means to be human in this world bum people out?

The great Japanese filmmaker Akira Kurosawa famously said, "To be an artist means never to avert one's eyes." How much toll does it take to not look away? Ecclesiastes says: "And I set my mind to know wisdom and to know madness and folly; I realized that this also is striving after wind. Because in much wisdom there is much grief, and increasing knowledge results in increasing pain."

At the same time, research, including a 2013 study by a neuroscientist at the University of Helsinki published in the *Proceedings of the National Academy of Sciences*, shows that babies begin learning in the womb; newborns not only recognize and prefer the sound of their mother's voice but the sounds and rhythms of the language she speaks. Babies actually cry in the accent of their mother; a German baby cries in a different pattern than a French or a Japanese child. Newborns also prefer the sounds their mother heard while pregnant, whether these sounds were pleasant (gentle songs, the roar of the ocean) or not (shrieking sirens or various soap opera themes). Likewise with tastes and smells. A baby whose mother ate licorice will like that taste at just days old, while one whose mother did not will turn away as if it were poison. Babies born to mothers who ate lots of chocolate are happier.

All of which means we come out of the womb not as blank canvases but already primed. Not only a mother's overall health and diet but also her stress levels—how anxious she is, how loved or unloved—pass on critical information to a fetus, laying down markers for what to expect from the world.

But there's even more than that. I am fascinated by (what I can understand of) the exploding field of behavioral epigenetics, which posits that the experiences of our recent ancestors leave molecular residue which adheres to their DNA— and therefore to ours. In other words, not just physical but psychological and even behavioral tendencies really can be inherited. If your grandmother or even your great-grandmother struggled with depression because she escaped from the Holocaust, or narrowly avoided a massacre in My Lai, or was enslaved and raped repeatedly or watched her father being lynched—or was simply neglected and unloved during childhood—it matters *to* you and *in* you. Whether you know it or not.

The Writer is fascinated by epigenetics. Eshu just laughs.

•

Late in the day on February 20, 2005, Hunter S. Thompson takes a gun to his head at Owl Farm, his compound in Woody

Creek, Colorado. His daughter-in-law and grandson, hearing the gunshot from the next room, mistake it for the sound of a falling book.

No More Games. No More Bombs. No More Walking. No More Fun. No More Swimming. Sixty-seven. That is seventeen years past fifty. Seventeen more than I needed or wanted. Boring. I am always bitchy. No Fun—for anybody. Sixty-seven. You are getting Greedy. Act your old age. Relax—This won't hurt.

•

Late July and I begin making a list of how the people I know would respond if I killed myself. This is in response to a friend who, when I call from the pit of my despair, says, "You can't kill yourself. So many people would be devastated if you did that."

This strikes me as ridiculous. There are not "so many people." Maybe a handful. I begin to count.

I create three categories and assign everyone I know:

Devastated.

Wow, what a bummer.

Wow, what a bummer, what's for lunch?

As might be expected, the vast majority of colleagues and acquaintances and friends and even some family members fall into either the second or the third category. In the first I place only my children, my mother and sisters and brother, a very dear friend. Eight people: more than many, less than some.

I fly to Washington, DC, with my daughter for her college orientation. I am hopeful that travel will turn things around, as it has sometimes in the past. A new perspective, a removal from the rut, the understanding that the world is much bigger than your petty issues and wounds. But after dropping my daughter off I find myself on the side of the road somewhere in northwest Washington, the hot sun beating through the window of the rental car as I sob as though my dog has just died. I stumble to a Panera, go inside for a cup of coffee, and pick up my phone.

For complicated reasons involving the recent retirement of my primary care physician and my health insurance HMO, it takes me twenty minutes, five phone calls, and no few tears to land an appointment with a psychiatrist, an appointment three weeks away. The last of several receptionists I speak to asks if I have immediate thoughts of harming myself. "Not for now," I tell her, hanging up.

Over the next few weeks, I frequently contemplate canceling the appointment. It feels both weak and useless to pursue a chemical solution to what, all my life, I have taken to be an issue of personality and temperament and lack of love. Part of me doesn't believe the pills will work. Part of me fears they will.

A week before the appointment I wake heavy-laden, freighted, and weary, the world's brutality chilling in my bones. I walk the dog and step in dog shit. I begin raking leaves in the yard and am promptly stung by wasps. Sobbing and despondent, I sit on the floor of my bedroom and call a friend who misunderstands the source of my agony ("just because you don't have a man?") and lectures me until I admit that I am silly and hang up. I take a Benadryl and crawl into bed.

When I wake two hours later the depression has broken: I know it the moment I open my eyes. It feels precisely like a fever that has crested, a seizure that has finally stopped. I am astonished at the sharp line of division. In the past the cloud has lifted slowly, imperceptibly, until one day I realized I stood again in the sun. It was never like this.

It is this strange, first-time demarcation, ironically, which keeps me from canceling the appointment. If a depression can break like a fever, maybe it *is* biological. And maybe some pills can save my life.

•

May 3, 1991. In his apartment in Manhattan Jerzy Kosiński drinks some booze, takes some drugs, wraps a plastic bag around his head.

I am going to put myself to sleep now for a bit longer than usual. Call it Eternity.

•

The shrink seems a little hurt when I say, in response to his question, that I chose him because he had the first available opening. He listens to my story with a distant gaze and a practiced half-smile of concern. At one point he stalls on a word and I provide it: enervating. He looks at me again.

He prescribes Wellbutrin. We discuss whether I should begin taking it right away or wait until the next episode, which might not come for weeks or even months—or, magically, never again. He warns that it takes time for antidepressants to become effective so that waiting is a risk, especially with winter (and an empty nest) coming on. I decide to wait, still hoping to muscle my way through. A few days later I feel the cloud descending again and panic. I call the shrink. He sends the script.

A friend tells me I will know when the drug kicks in because I will feel a few hours of intense happiness and energy. I do research and find out that this is common when starting Wellbutrin, so common it's called the Wellbutrin honeymoon. But my friend is a person who gets so excited at action movies she nearly leaps from her seat. I am fairly sure my biology will not react this way and I am right. I have no Wellbutrin honeymoon, no mania or giddy excitement. For a few nights I have trouble sleeping and my stomach hurts but otherwise life is the same. Except that slowly, slowly I begin to feel a perceptible evenness, a decided leveling out. It is palpable and definite and I am astonished. Is this what most people feel all the time?

I tell my close friends. Their reactions range. As with depression itself, everyone has an opinion on antidepressants and no one is reluctant to share. One friend asks if I have tried talk therapy first. Another says she hates "those things," that they are used because Americans don't like expressing their anger. I tell her expressing anger has never been a problem for me.

Two weeks in and I am no longer miserable. Is this really the drug? Irving Kirsch would say not. In *The Emperor's New Drugs* he argues that most, if not all, of the improvement people experience from antidepressants is due to placebo effect. One summary of the evidence argues that 25 percent of the observed benefit from antidepressants is due to a direct impact of the medication, 25 percent to spontaneous remission, and

50 percent to the placebo effect. Some researchers believe this means that antidepressants are very effective for treating people with severe depression but no better than placebo for those with mild- to-moderate depression.

All of which means what? Did I fit the imprecise criteria for major depression when I saw the shrink? Probably not. Did I fit it the week before? Possibly. All I know is that I have lived inside this brain for half a century and things have changed.

I enter the cage of my feelings and find them tempered, curled into the corner like obedient dogs. I poke around inside my mind/brain like an archaeologist, assessing the remains. Eshu is gone.

My mind before was full of dark places and sharp corners, wide valleys and glorious peaks. Okay, not that many peaks but the ones that were, were truly glorious, full of fury and insight and consciousness. In the flatness of this new landscape is all of that just gone? I wonder, interested and troubled, though troubled in a remote and distanced way. Because: drugs.

What really has changed? It's certainly not that life seems more meaningful than before. I still see no giant plan, no reason for everything that happens, no great truth uniting it all. Evil people still get away with evil deeds and good people still suffer, Wall Street hustlers are still rich and the kid I mentored at a school last week is still poor and struggling. War rages and people kill for idiotic reasons. And there is still no guarantee I will find love. So it goes, said Kurt Vonnegut. So it goes.

I guess all that's different is that when I'm depressed all these things feel overwhelming. But on the drugs they simply are what they are. So I stay on.

I have a few strange instances of stuttering. The first time it happens I am on the phone and I think, "Boy that was weird!" The second time I begin to freak out. Who begins stuttering in adulthood? Is this a brain tumor? Some other strange disease? It takes me a few days to make the connection: start a powerful new brain drug, start stuttering. Duh. I look it up: stuttering is a rare but not- unheard-of side effect of Wellbutrin. I call the shrink, who halves the dose. The stuttering decreases, then disappears.

•

Three weeks in and it's Saturday night and I am alone. Normally this would be painful. Normally the loneliness of my empty house and empty heart would be so bad my bones ached, so bad I'd want to chew off an arm. Tonight I am lonely but it's manageable. I step outside onto the porch and listen to the rain and for a second I smile. It's not so much that I feel actual gladness at being alive as that I realize I *should* feel gladness at being alive, and since I don't feel suffocating despair I am able, at least, to mimic happiness. Fake it till you make it. Welcome to America.

I go back inside and turn on the TV. PBS is playing Simon and Garfunkel's Concert in Central Park. I stand in my living room and listen to Paul Simon sing poetry about being forsaken and alone and I prepare to dissolve into a puddle of loneliness. But I don't. I stand there and sing along and it's as if my emotions are just out of reach. I can *see* sadness and despair, *see* their sharp, familiar faces but only from a distance. They're on the other side of the river, jumping up and down and waving but there's no bridge between us. They cannot cross.

Is that good? Is that a good and normal thing? It feels somehow false, a simulacrum of living. A simulacrum of the emotions and depth I used to have. The Writer is ambivalent. Though, yeah, I know how that sounds: *poor Kim, feeling sad that she's not as sad as she used to be.*

Better living through chemistry.

The next morning, a Sunday, the sadness returns. A wave of despondency descends as I remember that I'm alone not only in my house but in the world, that no matter how prettily I write or prettily I dress no one will ever really give a good god-damn. The tears come, the first in over a month. And then, like a train on the Red Line, they just stop. The waves of existential loneliness recede. I feel them go. I get dressed and take my dog Stella for a walk in the drizzle. She pauses every half block to sniff the grass.

This wave of despair will return randomly over the next few months, sometimes fleeting, sometimes strong enough to knock me down for an hour or two, but always growing lighter. When a woman is on certain versions of the Pill and the estrogen is insufficient she may bleed in between her periods. Gynecologists call this "breakthrough bleeding." I come to think of these periods of despair as breakthrough depression.

•

One year in now and the evenness holds. It occurs to me that this is a kind of Stella-like levelness, not unintelligent but circumscribed. Stella thinks of food when she's hungry and water when she's thirsty and sleep when she needs to sleep, and whatever emotional highs or lows that pass through her head are fleeting. Her needs are easily met, even her need for love and understanding (pet, scratch, hug, go away now), and whatever is happening in Syria or Missouri or the prisons of America or even in the other room is irrelevant to her happiness. Some people might consider this admirable. Stella is either the ultimate Buddhist or the ultimate American.

I do not mean to romanticize depression, and certainly not to romanticize suicide. Suicide devastates those left behind, a tornado through the heart I have seen in my family and among the children of friends. I do not mean to romanticize depression but neither do I mean to demonize it, or at least not to demonize mine. To demonize my depression is to diminish the last thirty-odd years of my life. To diminish both the suffering and the surviving, the pain and what crawled up from that pain. I do not mean to demonize my depression. Only, for my children, I mean to survive.

Still, sometimes I wonder. All those years of muscling, the endless days and weeks and months of toughing it out: did they make me a better person, strengthen my moral or emotional fortitude? Would I have written more novels without Eshu hovering, or fewer? Better novels or worse? Would literature mean as much to me? Would I be kinder or a total asshole? Would I still love James Baldwin like I love my life?

After a year on Wellbutrin I weaned myself without issue; two years later and all is well. There is research to suggest that once a person has been lifted from the chasm of major depression things like meditation and exercise can help prevent a tumble back into the abyss. Or maybe time, that ultimate of all medications, will lend a hand. From here I can almost see my sixties, when statistics predict that depression among women begins to drop.

If that does not happen for me I will just have to risk the return of Eshu. When he comes, if he comes, at least I'll know what to do: take up my pen.

•

Hart Crane, who leapt off a ship:
Goodbye, everybody!

Maurice's Blues

In late May my sister calls. Her son Maurice is being sentenced in Kansas City on June twenty-third. The charge is armed robbery. She needs to go, but does not want to go alone.

I stand in my kitchen, waiting for water to boil so I can make green tea. It's a beautiful late-spring afternoon, and I like my kitchen on such days: it's sunny and comfortable and warm. Also old, which does not bother me. The tile dates from the previous owner, who had a love affair with dusty pink. The picture window no longer opens, the cabinets are dark and unappealing, and the floor is actual linoleum. Through the open side window comes the sound of buzzing saws. A neighbor is renovating her kitchen for the second time since I have lived in this leafy little suburb; somebody died and left her a wad of cash. Across the way another neighbor is refinishing his attic, and on the next block up a dumpster sits in a driveway, collecting construction mess. In towns like this there's a constant churn of improvements, additions, refurbishments. On the outside my house looks the same as the others. Inside the best I can do is patch whatever breaks.

"What day is the twenty-third?" I ask my sister. I don't want to go to Kansas City. I don't want to attend a sentencing, to see my thirty-four-year-old nephew in chains.

"A Monday."

I have no viable excuse. By then my semester will be over, my luxurious summer leave well begun. My children are teenagers and old enough to take care of themselves for a night. If the trip takes longer than that they can stay with their father and his wife. The airfare is steep but it won't break me, though it would have bankrupted my mother. I can put it on my credit card.

I pour boiling water into my mug and the steam rises, the sharp scent of lemons prickling my nose. "Let me check on flights."

It will end up being a busy summer. In June there are two trips: first an East Coast college tour with my daughter, and then Missouri, where I sit in a dim and chilly courtroom to watch my nephew be sentenced to prison for the rest of his life.

No. Not the rest of his life, it only feels that way when the words "twenty-five years" smash down upon us. The judge, distracted or bored, mumbles the sentence, and it is as if my nephew's life has just ended, as if they've put him down like a dog.

In July I'll drive my daughter to the Rhode Island camp where she is a junior counselor, then take my son to New Hampshire for a walk around the campus of the boarding school he will attend in the fall. In August the three of us will spend a few days at a friend's condo on the Outer Banks. Also in August, Michael Brown will walk down a street in Ferguson, Missouri. A few minutes later he will be shot six times by Officer Darren Wilson. His body will lie in the street for four hours while his mother looks on.

Michael Brown was eighteen years old and six-four, broad

shouldered and chubby, baby faced and brown skinned. He was born to teenaged parents, neither of whom attended college. They later divorced, but remained deeply involved in his life. Brown struggled in high school but managed to graduate; he was heading to technical school when he was killed. He lived in a suburb of St. Louis that is 67 percent Black and has a 25 percent poverty rate.

When Michael Brown was killed, my son was fourteen years old and six feet tall, broad-shouldered and long limbed, as thin and lanky as licorice. His father and I were in our thirties when he was born, both college graduates; his father, who is white and holds a PhD, has remained closely involved in his life despite our divorce. My son grew up in a suburb of Boston that is 20 percent Black and has a 2.8 percent poverty rate.

I would like to believe these differences set my son apart from Michael Brown, that these facts serve as insulation, a sheet of Kevlar that will protect my child and keep him safe. I desperately want to believe that these differences project my son into some other America, one that never intersects with the America of Michael Brown. I want to believe these things but it would be foolish to do so. I am many things but I am not a fool.

"I read about it in the paper, in the subway, on my way to work," says the unnamed narrator of James Baldwin's story "Sonny's Blues". The "it" is his estranged brother's arrest and imprisonment. The two are alienated from each other because Sonny is a musician and heroin addict, while the narrator has become a teacher and family man, a law-abiding and upstanding citizen safely removed, he hopes, from the drugs, poverty, and nihilistic despair that have ensnared so many in their corner of Harlem. It is only after the narrator's daughter dies of polio that he is forced to confront not only his own suffering but the suffering of his brother as well, and also, by extension, the suffering of Black people in America. He is not and cannot be removed from that suffering, try as he might.

It had been a while since I'd seen Maurice, but in our family, large and far flung, that is not unusual. My mother raised five children in Memphis, a city she hated and could not wait to escape, and so we grew to hate it too. Memphis was poverty and struggle, and, as in quicksand, the more you fought, the faster and deeper you sank. The only real hope was to grab hold of something steady and haul yourself out. As adults my siblings and I have all moved far and often, setting down and ripping up roots in Florida, Pennsylvania, North Carolina, New York, New Hampshire, California, Washington, Maryland, Massachusetts, Texas, Missouri, South Korea, Scotland, and Germany. We are a family unafraid to begin again.

But the prize for emotional distance once belonged to me. When I was fifteen a white man appeared at my junior high school like some cut-rate fairy godfather and twinkled me away to boarding school. Poor Black kids tossed into rich white schools usually respond in one of three ways: they intensify their Blackness, assimilate into whiteness, or try to find some hopeless middle stance. I tried all three.

I joined the Afro-Exonian society and clung to the older Black girls. I cursed my kinky hair and ample hips. I dated a white guy who hung with the Black kids and had a Black stepfather. I changed my speech. I immersed myself in

African-American literature and acted in a production of *For Colored Girls Who Have Considered Suicide, When The Rainbow Is Enuff*—a role which may have saved my life. From the distance of a thousand miles I saw clearly not only all the things wrong with Memphis, but all the things wrong with my family, all the things from which I needed to escape. I was out only for myself.

After three years at Phillips Exeter Academy and four at Duke, I barely knew my family and they barely knew me. During my twenties and early thirties I maintained a polite, selfish remoteness from them all. I don't even remember when, precisely, Michelle married and moved to Missouri with her husband and three children, including Maurice. I didn't even meet the husband until the birth of their first child. On the rare occasions that I saw my nieces and nephews I hugged them and cooed over their childish paintings and clapped at their clumsy dancing, then went back to my life.

As for Maurice, I thought of him, when I thought of him at all, as the sweet, open-faced eleven-year-old I'd once watched play basketball in the driveway of my brother's house. That day, when I asked him what he wanted to be when he grew up he said, "I'm gonna be in the NBA." His father was small-statured, and so was Maurice, so I asked about his backup plan. He shrugged. "A fireman, I guess."

•

These are the facts of the case, as recorded in Maurice's appellate brief. On January 12, 2012, in Raymore, Missouri, two people robbed a Sonic Drive-In restaurant, while a third person acted as getaway driver. The Sonic was equipped with a video recording device. As security footage reveals, there was no way to identify the two robbers, fully cloaked, unidentifiable, but one of them snagged his belt in the store, and it came off. Later, authorities were able to garner DNA material from the belt, which, when tested, led them to arrest and detain a man named D. Black. (I have changed names here.) Mr. Black was arrested, at which point his girlfriend, Blanche White, contacted the tips hotline and reported to police that she had information implicating two other men in the Sonic heist: E. Blue and Maurice. She also identified a third individual as being involved, "Pinky." Then, after meeting with police on several occasions, Ms. White changed her story and fingered her boyfriend, Mr. Black, and Maurice as the perps, admitting she had hoped to deflect attention from her boyfriend. Finally, in early June 2012, she admitted to being the getaway driver. At trial, Ms. White said she has been diagnosed with several psychological illnesses, including bipolar disorder, manic anxiety, depression, and post-traumatic stress disorder, for which she is medicated.

At the time of the Sonic heist, Ms. White had known Maurice for approximately six months. She'd met him while visiting another inmate in the Western Missouri Correctional Center at Cameron, where Maurice was serving six years for "armed criminal action." Upon Maurice's release the two struck up a friendship and Ms. White permitted Maurice to stay overnight at her apartment a few nights per week; she drove him places occasionally, such as to get a driver's license and to enroll in college. She later lent him use of her vehicle, a Cadillac Deville. The last time this happened, Jackson County Sheriff's

Deputy Bryce Henderson (name not changed) pulled Maurice over and arrested him; there were several outstanding warrants for his arrest. Henderson claimed to have found a silver-and-Black handgun, loaded with "jacketed hollow points," in the car, with other bullets rolling loose on the floor. Maurice vehemently denied ownership or even knowledge of the gun, and subsequent DNA tests found no evidence linking him to it. Nor was any evidence found connecting the gun to the robbery. Deputy Henderson also claimed to have found bullets in Maurice's backpack. Ms. White was charged with first degree robbery and armed criminal action. After spending five and a half months in the Cass County Jail, she cut a plea bargain to a single count of second-degree robbery and received a five-year sentence, suspended. The prosecution offered her that deal on the condition that she testify against Maurice and Mr. Blue, which she did. This was the entirety of the evidence.

"Maurice should request a bench trial," said his lawyer. "No judge would ever convict on such scanty and contradictory evidence."

•

For my children, the question of college was never whether they were going, but where, an expectation as basic as learning to swim. I was only the second in my family to go to college, after my sister Benita. But college attendance stretches back much further in my ex-husband's family; his three sisters all hold advanced degrees and so do most of their children. This legacy stemmed not from great wealth—my former father-in-law was a high-school science teacher—but from access to the building blocks of the American Dream for the white middle class: some modest financial backing from my mother-in-law's family, a wealth-building house in a stable, non-redlined Philadelphia suburb, and the GI Bill.

The GI Bill, formally the Servicemen's Readjustment Act of 1944, offered returning soldiers subsidized vocational training, stipends for college and trade-school tuition, help with living expenses, and low-interest mortgages. But the legislation was not nearly the success for Black soldiers that it was for their white counterparts. Southern congressmen pressed (and northern congressmen agreed) to have the programs administered by local officials rather than the federal government, which led to inequitable treatment for the nearly seventy thousand Black veterans pouring into the labor force. As Ira Katznelson documents in *When Affirmative Action Was White*, qualified African-Americans were denied housing and business loans, denied admission to predominantly-white colleges and trade schools, and excluded from job-training programs in up-and-coming fields like radio and electrical work. Meanwhile, Black veterans who could access their benefits were often channeled toward underfunded and overwhelmed Black colleges. According to Katznelson, in 1946 white people held 86 percent of the skilled and semiskilled nonfarm jobs available in Mississippi, while 92 percent of the unskilled jobs went to Blacks.

Nor was the discrimination limited to the South: "fewer than one hundred of the sixty-seven thousand mortgages insured by the GI Bill in New York and New Jersey," Katznelson writes, "went toward home purchases by nonwhites."

As far as I can piece together, my mother's two uncles both served in the U.S. Army during the Korean War. As far as my mother recalls, neither one of them went to college, although she thinks my great Uncle Dempsey did attend some kind of agricultural school. Both secured steady public-sector jobs and built themselves modest middle-class lives. Their sister, my grandmother, never finished high school and worked mostly as a domestic.

My mother, who thirsted for education and always wanted more, managed to propel herself into Knoxville College, but could not find the money or support necessary to finish her degree. My father joined the Navy after high school, then drove a truck.

How many generations does it take to lift a family? What if that family is Black? Among my mother's five children there are four college degrees and a couple of master's degrees, but only half of my nieces and nephews have continued on this college path. Is this failure? Is this success? What is the goal for a Black family in America? What is possible? No one in my family is on public assistance. Maurice alone suffocates in jail.

•

My sister's plane from Maryland is delayed, so I stroll the airport to pass the time. I spot at least a dozen cops wearing Kevlar vests and carrying semiautomatic rifles, as well as a pair of K9 patrols. I try to remember the last time I saw guard dogs at Logan, which probably handles more flights in an hour than Kansas City International does all day.

At a snack bar I grab a bag of chips, but when the cashier says, "That will be $2.50," I return them to their basket with a laugh.

The cashier is a Black woman, maybe forty, with round glasses and relaxed hair. She gives me a look that says, *Girl, yes, that noise is ridiculous, I can't even barely bring myself to say it and I'm glad you put those chips back because I would have wondered about you.* Aloud she says, "I got you." And when I leave she comes after me offering a bag of Lay's she has taken from her lunch.

"Oh, no!" I protest, but she insists, and, because I have learned to accept kindness when it is offered, I give in. "God bless you," I say. I take my snack and head to my sister's gate. She steps off the plane looking weary. I give her a hug.

The young brother at the rental car office fans his new diamond earrings and makes fun of his friend's cubic zirconia. It kicks Kansas City up a notch in my estimation that a kid so unabashedly gay can live here openly; I'd have expected a young man like that to get the hell out of town at the first opportunity. Then again, the South, of which Missouri is sort of a part, has always been more tolerant of individuals (if not groups) than the self-righteous North would ever understand.

My sister turns to me as we leave the airport, mentions her ex-husband. "I told him it was the biggest mistake to move here," she says. I nod.

My eldest sister is also my kindest sibling. Not surprisingly, she was the most wounded by my parents' divorce and our father's subsequent disappearance from our lives. At least, that's my armchair analysis of her struggles—running after useless men in a yearning search for love. In her essay "In Search of Our Mothers' Gardens," Alice Walker writes brilliantly about the creativity of Black women in a racist patriarchy: "When we have asked for love, we have been given children. In short, even our plainer gifts, our labors of fidelity and love, have been knocked down our throats." My sister loved her children as best she could; she found God and got saved; she married an Air Force man who styled himself a lay minister and had two more children; she moved with her husband to be near his family and sent her children to Christian schools. What went wrong? I don't know. Maybe nothing.

The day is hot, humid, and overcast, the sky the color of laundry lint. It's an hour's drive to where we're going, and we're late. There are highways everywhere, interstates looping up and over one another like the Hot Wheels tracks my brother played with as a boy. When I'm in Boston I forget how sprawling a city can be, how much wide, flat, sky-touching space there is in America. In New England we live narrow, compacted lives.

The Cass County Justice Center rises in the middle of a field just off Highway 71 in Harrisonville, massive, blocky, and bland, a soulless building for the soulless work being conducted inside. There are three main entrances, each helpfully labeled in giant block letters:

JUSTICE CENTER. SHERIFF'S OFFICE. JAIL.

Cass County, I will come to learn, is not KC. Kansas City's population is 60 percent white, 30 percent Black, with 19 percent of its residents living below the poverty line. Some 13 percent of the 35,000-odd local businesses are Black owned. There are 1,459 people per square mile. Cass County's population is just over a hundred thousand and enjoys a poverty rate below 8 percent. There are fewer than one hundred fifty people per square mile, and the number of Black-owned businesses was too negligible for the Census to count. Cass County is also 93 percent white. For a Black man in America, this is never a good thing.

My sister tells me to leave my cell phone in the car: recording devices are not allowed in the courthouse. No doubt there are legitimate safety reasons for this, but if there is one thing we have learned from recent summers of videotaped police killings, it is that power prefers to operate in the dark.

In the parking lot we meet my sister's former father-in-law, who has also come to bear witness. Maurice calls this man "Grandfather," though they are not biologically related, and the man accepts both the name and the responsibility. He is of medium height, thin and muscular, with the rough-hewn strength of someone who has worked with his body all his life. My sister hugs him. He smiles sadly and shakes his head.

Inside the courthouse we pass through metal detectors under the watchful eyes of four deputies: three men, one stout woman, all white. I take their temperature, try to gauge their level of itchy-fingered fear. I do this without really meaning to, without consciously thinking about it. My sister offers them the same sweet and open smile she gives to everyone. I give off the *don't-think-I'm-intimidated-by-you* vibe I feel in such circumstances. The guards wave us through.

Inside, the building is surprisingly modern and bright:

blond wood and pale walls, with large windows and skylights that let in the sun. No pillars or heavy wooden doors like the courthouses of New England, no inscriptions about justice etched into the walls. No statues of Lady Justice, blind and balancing the scales.

We climb the wide central staircase to the second floor, and as we pass people ascending and descending it's pretty easy to tell who's here for work and who's here to have their life destroyed. Who's swinging a briefcase? Who's clutching her purse? Who's discussing lunch options or pumping a colleague's hand? Which faces are stitched with fear?

Judge Michael R. Wagner of the 17th Judicial Circuit is already seated when we arrive. He sits at a bench far removed from the gallery, so far away I can barely make out his face or expression. He does not address the subdued, submissive people hunched in the room, leaving that to his strutting, barking bailiff. The gallery is filled with all races of people. Everyone on the other side of the bar, with the exception of the defendants, is white.

The first hearing we witness is conducted in lowered, inaudible voices, the attorneys and the white defendant gathered around the judge's bench. At first I think this is simply a sidebar, but then it becomes clear the entire hearing will be conducted this way. And then the one after, and the one after that. I am astonished, having never witnessed such secrecy at the many trials I have covered as a reporter.

After nearly two hours, it is our turn. The judge signals to the bailiff, who opens a door to the holding area and leads Maurice out. He is dressed in an orange jumpsuit, his head lowered, his feet shackled and his hands in chains. He can't look at his mother and it shreds my heart to look at him.

Maurice is led to the stand. The judge conducts business in such low tones that we can hear nothing. I sit in the audience, boiling with fury. If this is not blatantly against the law it is certainly and blatantly against democracy. When Maurice's attorney waddles back to us I ask him, "What's going on?"

"It's not good."

He starts to say more, but the bailiff, a puffed-up little man with leathery skin and a slicked-back pompadour, has already reprimanded the crowd for making noise. The attorney leads us outside. Beads of perspiration dimple his forehead and the space between his nose and upper lip.

"It's not good," he says again, as if we do not know this already. "Not good at all."

Contrary to what the attorney had assured us, the judge was not going to rule out the testimony of the girlfriend, despite her contradictions and admitted lies. Any reasonable jury of Maurice's peers would have found that testimony not credible and certainly not beyond a reasonable doubt, but the judge lets it stand.

When Maurice was charged with armed robbery in 2005, my sister did not scramble to raise money for a private attorney. A devout Christian, she believed her son was guilty of that crime and should face the consequences of his actions. As a family, we followed her lead.

This time is different. My sister believes her child when he says he did not do it. In the weeks before the trial, I sit in my comfortable suburban house in Massachusetts and read the court documents and am bewildered that it has come to this. I share them with a lawyer friend, who sighs and shakes his head. "Missouri," he says.

I do not know whether Maurice is innocent. I do know the prosecutor's case is thin, jerry-rigged, and shot full of reasonable doubt. I also know that Blacks and whites receive disparate treatment at every stage of the criminal justice system, from stops and searches, to prosecutions and arrests, to trials and sentencing. I know that nationally, Black men are incarcerated in state prisons at a rate five times that of white men. And I know that convictions for similar federal crimes lead to twenty percent longer prison sentences for Black men than for whites.

Maurice's lawyer professes shock at the turn of events. We can appeal, of course, if we can raise the money for representation, but it is much harder to successfully appeal a judge's ruling than a jury's verdict. As the legal resource organization Justia notes, the appellate court can overturn, or retry, a lower court's decision if it finds that a jury committed "reversible error": a mistake that changed the outcome of the trial. A verdict handed down by a lower-court judge, however, is reviewed only for "abuse of discretion," meaning that the judge acted unreasonably in reviewing the evidence. How often does a panel of judges conclude that a fellow judge abused his or her power? I don't know: state-by-state comparisons of criminal court adjudication and appellate rates are difficult to find. My guess is: not very often.

At some point along the way—I'm not sure—Maurice was likely offered a plea bargain. All across America, in both federal and state courts, the vast majority of cases are resolved through this process. According to the *New York Times*, in 1980, 81 percent of federal convictions were reached through guilty pleas. In 2013: 97 percent. Legal experts blame congressional sentencing guidelines and mandatory minimum sentences, which transferred nearly unchecked power to prosecutors and discouraged defendants from going to trial. Of the more than nineteen hundred people exonerated in the U.S. since 1989, *15 percent* were in prison because they pleaded guilty to the crime of which they were accused. And a 2017 review of two thousand cases by the National Registry of Exonerations found that Black people convicted of violent crimes are significantly more likely than their white counterparts to be later exonerated.

I don't know whether Maurice is innocent. I do know the whole system stinks.

I wish I knew my nephew better, though, as a man, and that he knew me and my children, and that the knowing might have made a difference. I remember him mostly as he was as a child: his silliness, his talent at drawing, the way he laughed. In the months that follow, I write to him, tell him he is not forgotten. I send him books. I don't know if he reads them, but he writes in return, his letters full of anguish and guilt at being absent from his young daughter and for having hurt his mother. He expresses plans to appeal his case, their grandiosity proportional to their hopelessness. A friend who was once incarcerated tells me that obsessing over one's case is common among prisoners. "What else do you have to focus on?" he asks. "What else will keep you sane?"

•

The rest of it, quickly: Maurice's hanging head as they guide him, shackled—fucking shackled!—from the stand. My sister's face as we walk, numb, next door to the Sheriff's Department to speak to Maurice before we leave. The strange, smiling kindness of the woman behind the glass: she signs us in and directs us to plastic chairs, to our vigil. My shattering heart as I enter the "visiting" room and realize I will not even get to see my nephew in person, only through a fuzzy Black-and-white television screen. If this is not criminal I do not know the meaning of the word. The disinfectant smell of the heavy Black phone that I hold to my ear. The sound of Maurice crying as he hides his face from the camera. The heavy, wet feeling of love in my mouth as I urge him to *hold on, hold on, hold on.*

On the ride back to the airport, my sister is solemn, stoic. My chest feels constricted. We grab a sandwich. I am reluctant to trickle even this small amount into the Missouri economy, but a body has to eat. I put my sister on the plane back to her home state, and wait for deliverance.

Why did my sister want me to come to Missouri? To bear witness? Or from some faint hope that I could prevent, or at least moderate, the inevitable? Some hope that my list of accomplishments—professor, writer, occasional television host—might stall the relentless machine. Some hope we that could show an uncaring judge that Maurice was not just another nigger to be tossed onto the garbage heap.

As my plane takes off, I realize I shared that foolish hope, that misplaced belief that my degrees and accomplishments— my proofs of entry, my stamped and dated visas to the world of Whiteness and Acceptability—might somehow sway the judge. When my sister first called, I sat down and composed a long, impassioned letter to the judge, outlining our history, accepting our responsibility, throwing Maurice and all of us upon the mercy of the court. Did the judge bother to read it? I don't know; he neither mentioned it nor allowed us to speak on Maurice's behalf. I think of the letter from the father of the white Stanford University student convicted of rape, how the father lamented that his son's "happy-go-lucky" personality had been altered by "events," how he asked the judge not to penalize his son for "twenty minutes of action." That judge handed down six months in jail. Maurice's judge handed down twenty-five years.

None of which is to say Maurice didn't hand society the gun with which to shoot him. And the bullets, too.

I put my sister on her plane home with her heart permanently broken, and board mine carrying only the blues of the One Who Thinks She Got Away. Why do some people escape and others fall behind? Why are some people able to swim to safety (or what they think is safety) while others struggle? Who gets a seat on the lifeboat and who is allowed to drown?

"Sonny's Blues" contains an extended flashback in which the narrator's mother tells him that he must look out for his brother if something ever happens to her. The narrator, anxious to escape the conversation so he can visit his girlfriend, tells his mother that Sonny will be fine because he's a good boy with good sense.

'It ain't a question of his being a good boy,' Mamma said. 'Nor of his having good sense. It ain't only the bad ones, nor yet the dumb ones that gets sucked under.'

Flying over America I try to push Maurice from my mind. My daughter needs a dentist's appointment and a drive to the mall; my son must have his braces removed. There are textbooks to order and luggage to pack and forms to sign. The narrator of "Sonny's Blues" puts his brother out of mind too, until his own daughter's death—and the memory of his mother's warning—makes a lie of his belief in safety, both as a Black man and as a human being.

Back home in Boston my daughter frets over her coming senior year. "The pressure," she says, "is ridiculous."

Fire, All the Time

A few months ago I was given a book by a suitor: *Anger* by the great Buddhist monk Thich Nhat Hahn.

"What's this?" I asked.

"A gift," he said, sliding it across the dinner table.

"What kind of shitty gift is a book about controlling my anger?" I yelled. "Fuck you!"

Little joke. I didn't really say that.

What I really did was to smile ruefully and thank him and take the book home and toss it on the shelf, because who really wants to read a book about their baggage? Who wants to face that stuff?

It's been a long and complicated relationship, me and anger. We met at Exeter when I was fifteen, though, now that I think about it he'd probably been stalking from the alleys long before then. At Exeter he came right up and offered his hand. "This place, this world, these people do not mean for you to live," he whispered. "You can go along and die. Or you can get pissed." Easy choice, no choice, though even then I felt the double edge of that sword, slicing away and toward. Anger was safe and energizing and life-saving, yes, life-saving. Also isolating, enervating. Dangerous.

I don't remember being that angry in college; it took a few

years for the palpable relief of having survived Exeter to wear off. Also, Duke was a good school then but not nearly the competitive powerhouse it is today: all the "you're-only-here-because-you're-Black" shit was kept to a minimum. Even when it did arise it felt somehow less threatening; after Exeter I pretty much knew I could hang.

Out in the real world after graduation Dude Anger reappeared. I was a working journalist, pinballing from murder scenes to school board meetings and project shootings and hearings at city hall and for the first time I began to develop a sociological understanding of what had happened and was happening yet to Black people in America. The (CIA-supported) crack epidemic and the draconian War on Drugs. The re-segregation of the public schools and the debate over property tax funding. All sorta history I'd never, ever learned in school. The more poverty I covered the more poverty I understood, and anger shoved aside the overwhelming and debilitating shame of having been poor myself. In the stunted lives of the people I wrote about I saw my own family, its (partial) narrow escape, other people I knew. Then I crossed the tracks and listened to white politicians gush over Ronald Reagan, hold up George Bush. It was morning in America but only for some people. Then I went back to the newsroom and heard angry, resentful white reporters whisper I was only there because I was Black.

Here's a story: I wrote my first novel thinking it was about all kinda things: journalistic exploitation, the struggle of post-civil rights Black people caught between two worlds, love, coming-of-age, etc. At the first stop on my book tour a radio interviewer asked me, before the interview, for a five-second summation of the book's theme. I couldn't do it, so she offered one herself. "Seems to me this book is about anger, and how even righteous anger is ultimately self-destroying," she said.

"Holy Moly!" I said. "You're right! I wish I had known that when I was writing the book."

"Well . . . the book opens with the protagonist slapping a white female colleague," she said. "That might have been a clue."

James Baldwin said, "To be a Negro in this country and to be relatively conscious is to be in a rage almost all the time." When I discovered the scalpel-sharp anger of James Baldwin I felt myself to be in excellent company. Sometimes I wonder why more people aren't angry. Sometimes I wonder how so many people can live in this world, can look around at the raging injustices and inequities of our society and not be fricking furious. Sometimes I wonder what the hell is wrong with y'all. I mean, hello!

Still, there are costs to anger, external and internal, political and personal. Critics accused James Baldwin of being bitter, used this accusation to dismiss his stinging truth telling, his prophetic calls. Uncle Jimmy was sho-nuff angry but he was never bitter and he did not despair. He was, in fact, angry precisely because he refused to give in and give up, to settle into cynical apathy or self-interested privilege . "I don't think I'm in despair. I can't afford despair. I can't tell my nephew, my niece . . . You can't tell the children there's no hope."

The external costs to anger are not important, but the internal and the interpersonal ones are. Fire a rocket at the monster and the shrapnel may take out an innocent bystander. Or even someone you really care about.

I dug out that stupid book and started reading it. (Thank you former suitor! Hope all is well! Big smile!) I will never become a Great Being, an enlightened one. I will probably never completely let go of my anger, in part because I don't want to. But between here and there lies a whole world of possibilities, a way of making peace with the fire inside.

Thich Nhat Hanh writes, "If your house is on fire, the most urgent thing to do is go back and try to put out the fire, not to run after the person you believe to be the arsonist. If you run after the person you suspect has burned your house, your house will burn down while you are chasing him or her. This is not wise."

Well, yeah. When you put it that way. All right.

Victim and Victor
Both Start with *V*

The truth is, I couldn't bring myself to watch that first strange meeting.

I knew President Obama would rise to the occasion, would do what needed to be done. But I didn't want to see it, didn't want to see him humbled, didn't want to watch a dignified and decent president, the first Black one the United States has known, forced to welcome a race-baiting demagogue to the People's House.

But one can only turn so long from history.

So when Obama held a post-election press conference a few days after the 2016 election, I poured myself a glass of wine and buckled up, prepared to be depressed. But no—Obama came out smiling. Not the forced grimace of the defeated nor the smirk of the victor but a warm and genuine smile. He joked with the press corps about their question-stacking habits and spoke movingly about the death of journalist Gwen Ifill. He covered issues ranging from Syria to climate change, and for over an hour fielded questions about the election, the state of the nation, the president-elect. He calmly and understatedly made clear the difference between the man going out and the man coming in:

"This office is bigger than any one person. And that's why

ensuring a smooth transition is so important. It's not something that the Constitution explicitly requires, but it is one of
those norms that are vital to a functioning democracy—similar to norms of civility and tolerance, and a commitment to
reason and facts and analysis. It's part of what makes this country work. And as long as I'm president, we are going to uphold
those norms and cherish and uphold those ideals."

Hey, what's the temperature there, in the presidential
shade?

What was most striking during that hour-long exercise
in leadership and maturity was not his steadiness, his tact and
diplomacy in the face of defeat. What was most striking was
just how undefeated Barack Obama really was.

Of all the accomplishments of Michelle and Barack
Obama, individually and together, this may have been their
greatest: They left the White House not only strong, but actually stronger than when they entered. All visible evidence
pointed to two people utterly centered, at perfect peace with
themselves, each other and their place in history.

We saw Michelle's ease as she oversaw the arrival of the
White House Christmas tree that year, or as she shushed yet
another desperate voter calling for her to run for president. We
saw her joke with James Corden and dance with Jimmy Fallon.
Saw her going peacefully to bed on Election Night: "Once you
do what you can do, you rest easy. It was in the hands of the
American people. Anything I felt about the election, I said, and
I stand by." We saw her leave the White House more toned,
more glamorous, and utterly, utterly self-assured.

We saw Barack smile as he serenaded a child dressed like

Prince for Halloween. Saw him stand side-by-side with Angela Merkel, world leaders on the world stage. Saw him politely welcome the man who unrelentingly and unceasingly promoted lies about his birth.

We saw the Obamas' easy self-assurance despite eight years not only of Republican political obstruction, but personal vilification. Saw their glowing contentment despite a relentless questioning of their legitimacy as citizens, as leaders— and most pointedly as representatives of the United States. Saw their Gibraltar-like centeredness despite threats and public rantings, US congressmen screaming out "you lie" during a joint address, bumper stickers praying for their deaths, public officials comparing them to monkeys and apes, people working themselves into a frenzy because Michelle Obama pushed for healthier school lunches and reduced childhood obesity (Ted Cruz had promised that his wife would bring French fries back to school lunches if he was elected).

The Clintons left the White House embattled and defensive, grimly plotting their return. George H. W. Bush evacuated to Texas to lick his one-term wounds while his son, done but dampened, ambled home to paint, leaving behind a nation on the verge of economic collapse. Jimmy Carter retreated south of the Mason-Dixie line utterly defeated, though he later resurrected himself. Even mild-mannered Gerald Ford left Washington vanquished, too hoarse to give his concession speech, bowing his head to the anger at pardoning his crooked former boss. Only Ronald Reagan departed the furnace as sunny and raven-haired and Teflon-coated as he entered (despite the assassination attempt), but Teflon eventually deteriorates.

The Obamas were and are not Teflon. The Obamas are Lonsdaleite. Even as our nation convulses and writhes, a king snake biting itself, the Obamas stand calm. America may well be broken. The Obamas are not.

Of course it is this very unassailable, meteorite-hard sense of self that has for so long infuriated Obama's enemies. That sent the Joe Wilsons into paroxysms of anger. That rankled the Ted Nugents and made the small-town, public official racists in Indiana and Pennsylvania and West Virginia and Kentucky smack the send button on their ranting Facebook posts. Obama's sense of self rankles and frightens not because his enemies really believe he "has a deep-seated hatred of white people," (to quote a pre-enlightened Glenn Beck) but because they fear, deep in their little hearts, that Obama doesn't much care about white people either way. Which is to say: Michelle and Barack Obama clearly love and respect many human beings, including close friends and family members, who happen to be white (which sets them apart from the 75 percent of white Americans who report that their core social network includes no people of a race different from their own). But with whiteness itself they are unimpressed.

This is their real crime.

This is their real crime, and every Black American knows it: How many times have we ourselves stood accused. All it takes is a perceived "unfriendliness," a declined lunch invitation, a disinterest in being the Best Black Friend. I've been labeled angry, aloof, and even uppity at institutions from Phillips Exeter Academy to the *New York Times*, and not once could the people who really knew me understand the origins of such projections.

Once a friend (who happens to be white) pulled me aside at her dinner party to ask why the absent husband of one of the other guests had reacted with snarky anger to the mention of my name. I did not know this man, had never spoken to him, had seen him only in passing on the local school playgrounds and soccer fields. But he told my friend, "She walks around this town like she owns it!"

My friend was bewildered; she didn't know what he meant. But I knew. He meant I engaged that town and those people as though I belonged there, as though, in my confidence of my right to be, I could focus my attention where I liked. Which was not on him.

White America yearns to remain at the center of Black consciousness. What else was the post-Reconstruction creation of the Mammy archetype—sexless, soothing, utterly devoted to her enslavers—but a longing for the good old days when (it was believed) whiteness was the sun around which Blackness obediently revolved? What else are Black-white buddy films, the Best Black Friend in sitcoms, most of Morgan Freeman's career? What else are movies like the 2016 bomb *Mr. Church* and the 2011 hit (and 2009 bestseller) *The Help*? *The Help* is particularly instructive, the gift that gives again and again and again. In that movie Viola Davis's character, conveniently childless and manless, devotes her time and love (and some of the worst, most idiotic mimicry of Black vernacular English to rise on film) to the white daughter of her employer. The character played by Octavia Spencer is supposed to be a radical who tells her employers what she thinks of them, but in the end she not only compromises but actually debases her art—her cooking—to get back at one white employer. And the Cicely Tyson character dies of a broken heart because her white employer kicks her out.

Think about that for a moment. Here is a woman who lived her life under the boot of legalized white supremacy, enduring and surviving things far worse than not being able to piss where the white folks pissed. Here is a woman who managed to raise her daughter amidst this violence, educate her to know herself, send her north to a life of relative freedom in Chicago. Here is a woman who did all of that and she dies of a broken heart because the white woman she works for don't love her no more? What that says is that in this novel by a white woman, this white female character stood at the center of this Black woman's emotional and psychological life. Which is precisely where white America longs to be, one way or the other. The opposite of love is not hate, it's indifference. Indifference is what really stings.

In his great essay "Letter to My Nephew on the 100th Anniversary of the Emancipation Proclamation," James Baldwin wrote: "In this case the danger in the minds and hearts of most white Americans is the loss of their identity. . . Any upheaval in the universe is terrifying because it so profoundly attacks one's sense of one's own reality. Well, the Black man has functioned in the white man's world as a fixed star, as an immovable pillar, and as he moves out of his place, heaven and earth are shaken to their foundations."

The Obamas left Washington intact because they internalized none of the hatred which swirled around them. They were never victims, even when being viciously victimized. This may be their greatest legacy to us, if we allow it. We can all learn something from them. If it's not already too late.

•

For the past few years I've been trying to figure out how to react to the wave of protests by Black and brown students that have swept campuses across the United States, including my own, Emerson College. In 2015, when a group of about two hundred students of color and their allies marched out of class and into our faculty assembly to protest the campus racial climate my immediate reaction was weariness. For two hours they detailed the slights, diminishments, and moments of cultural and racial aggression they had experienced. For two hours they told of white students using "nigger" in the dining hall and swastikas scrawled on dorm room doors, of whitewashed syllabi and curriculum, of professors who ignored them or singled them out for "the Black Perspective" or made casually racist statements like, "The reason there's not more diversity in publishing is because Black people don't read."

Listening to the students I felt exhausted. None of what they said surprised me and none did I doubt: I knew they spoke the truth. The weariness came from knowing how much of what they recounted could have (and did) take place nearly verbatim during my own undergraduate days, decades past.

But what felt new, or at least different, was their reaction. Beneath the anger and frustration lay something else: a palpable woundedness. These students weren't just affected by the very real racial aggressions they listed, they were existentially threatened—and very vulnerable to that threat. "I'm broken," said one student. "Y'all broke me." Which hurt my heart but also made me wonder: *Why is that? Why are these young people broken in a way my grandmother, who grew up in the teeth of Jim Crow Mississippi, was not?*

Then another student said, in so many words, "I came to Emerson expecting to be accepted and nurtured and welcomed. I came here expecting to be loved." And the answer to my wondering was clear.

I wish to be careful here. It's easy for age to misremember the passions of youth, to muffle the grief of the past. It's even easier for age to stand atop the soap box and proffer wise and useless advice.

I wish to be careful because I don't want to give aid to the enemy, to hand a bullet to apologists who would rather shoot the crying children than stop the bullies causing them to cry.

I wish to be careful, but I am trying to remember if I ever went anywhere in educational or professional life, to boarding school or college, to one newsroom after another, to summer jobs and academia, expecting even to be welcomed, let alone loved. America of the 1970s and 1980s and 1990s was different than contemporary America—or at least that was what the children have been taught—but I'm trying to remember if I ever invested emotionally in *any* (corporate, white, American) institution the way these students apparently have.

It is the job of youth to be both hopeful and impatient, to expect better and be disappointed when better does not come. I want to tell these students to keep doing their job, but to keep work at work and not at home. I want to tell them not to stop fighting—they must fight, for us and for themselves—but to not be victimized.

President Obama took office during the worst financial and economic crisis since World War II and left office having righted the ship. Michelle Obama reinvigorated the office of First Lady, salvaging it both from the lovely irrelevancy of both Mrs. Bushes and the hackle-raising "co-presidency" of First Lady Hillary. Her campaign against childhood obesity and in favor of healthier eating transformed the American food landscape in ways not always visible. Her campaign for girls' education took her around the world. And her savvy use of celebrity to promote her initiatives set the standard for First Ladies to come.

For these accomplishments, and for the corresponding failures which all presidencies have, Obama and his wife received unprecedented heckling, abuse, obstruction, and vitriol, not only from random citizens but from elected officials and the Republican leadership.

Some argue the president should have been more direct in condemning the racism which rained down upon his head. Perhaps, though it is difficult to believe it would have done much good. Racism is as American as apple pie. It is the Obamas' reaction to that sweet poison I find most instructive, their calm, centered, not-taking-it-personally response from which I want my students, and myself, to learn.

Michelle Obama said, "When they go low, we go high," but it's more like: "When they go low, we first attempt to explain, calmly and with plenty of evidence, why going high is the better route. If that doesn't work, we give them a sympathetic pat on the back and go around."

I want to remind my students about the power of language, the power not only to dismantle systems of oppression but also to strengthen from within. To hold oneself as marginalized, as a victim of institutional racism and oppression, as a receiver of micro-aggressions, is to show up for the fight dressed in flammable clothes. To hold oneself as the Obamas do is to show up not only flawless but fireproof. As James Baldwin said, "It is experience which shapes a language; and it is language which controls an experience."

To be clear, this is not the same advice against "being offended" so disingenuously and hypocritically dished out by traditional conservatives and the blatant racists of the so-called "Alt Right." Disingenuous because it is ahistorical, feigning innocence of deeply-embedded power imbalances, pretending the objections of Black and brown students grow solely out of what someone said to them in class, not the very real threat those words (and the structures which underlie them) present. Hypocritical because no one in America cries wounded more loudly than the white folks—working class and college-educated—who lifted Trump to victory. No one stands more magically removed from lectures about personal responsibility in the face of unemployment or foreclosed homes, no one gets told less to "stop whining" and get another job. No one gets more top-level support in the nursing of resentments; even Obama bent over backward to pat the trembling shoulder. One white man I know mansplained to me, in the days immediately after the election, why Clinton had lost: because of Obama's "clinging to their guns and their religion" comment in 2008.

"People don't get over that kind of thing," he told me. But

when I pointed out that Black people are constantly told to get over 250 years of slavery, 100 years of legalized oppression and violence and second-class citizenship, and 50 more years of viscous blowback to every meager gain in human rights, he shut up.

White men calling Black students spoiled is like the specialist of all special snowflakes calling the pebble delicate.

Toni Morrison once told a story to *The Guardian*. She was fourteen or fifteen, working as a domestic in the home of a white woman in her hometown of Lorraine, Ohio. The woman yelled at Morrison for being useless. Morrison took it personally and ran home in distress. Her father gave her a stern lecture, one she never forgot, one which made her all-but-impenetrable to racist bullying, in school and beyond.

"He said, 'Go to work, get your money and come home. You don't live there.'"

In other words, said Morrison: You are not obliged to live in someone else's imagination of you. You're not even obliged to acknowledge it.

Where is home? Where do we live? Most Americans have no idea. A nation, a region, a state of blue or red. A race or a religion, a gender or an ethnic group. An *identity*. Here's how we do things in Texas. This is the real America. Welcome to Red Sox Nation. California, land of dreams. Most Americans stomp around in one or two small and bolted rooms believing they are home. Believing they *know* where they live when they've never left the doorway. Never examined the foundation. Never been upstairs, or to the kitchen, or to the den ... But why belabor the metaphor?

All these places, all these rooms, are important. All these places, all these rooms are utterly irrelevant. Real home is the knowledge of these truths. Toni Morrison said she never took drugs because she wanted to feel what she felt. "Even if it's not happiness, whatever that means. Because you're all you've got."

The Obamas know.

On Self-Delusion

The last time I lied to myself was five years ago, when I pretended a man loved me who most certainly did not. By *pretended* I don't mean I stalked him from the shadows or play-acted meeting his mother or secretly tattooed his initials to my thigh. I didn't try to stop myself from raging at his crappy behavior; I made no lame, half-hearted excuses to my friends.

What I did was to simply go on seeing a person who treated my heart like toilet paper, who valued my soul and my very being about as much as he valued Styrofoam. I pretended to be in charge of what was happening. I told myself that even though I wanted more I could accept less and not be compromised, that the excitement and the sex were worth it, at least for a while. I told myself I was not trying to win his love. I told myself I knew I never would.

One big ball of lies, intertwined and interlocked. It took a long time to unravel the ball, to stretch it out and examine from end to end but finally I managed to do so. I have not lied to myself since. Unless, of course, I have. Unless telling myself I do not lie to myself is the biggest lie of all.

In her 1961 essay "On Self-Respect," Joan Didion suggests that it is easier to fool others than to fool ourselves. "Most of our platitudes notwithstanding, self-deception remains the most difficult deception. The charms that work on others count for nothing in that devastatingly well-lit back alley where one keeps assignations with oneself: no winning smiles will do here, no prettily drawn lists of good intentions."

As much as I admire Didion, I'm afraid I must disagree. It seems to me that most of us live our lives in a state of self-deception, a state the size of Texas and California combined. Some people patrol the borders of their states, eyeing the fence and perhaps occasionally making a run for it. Others never even come close to the border, living instead deep within their home-land, never wondering or wandering.

Most of our platitudes notwithstanding, self-deception remains the most common of deceptions. We spend our days not so much lying to others as simply trying to get them to swallow what we ourselves have already desperately choked down. Didion, who was only twenty-seven when she wrote "On Self-Respect," saw this better as she aged;[1] that she did not see it earlier is probably not unrelated to her societal position, which is to say: cushioned, privileged, white. (Note the unquestioned beliefs about birthright and Manifest Destiny underlying the essay. Note the purely metaphorical use of "Indians"—the peoples, not the word.)

James Baldwin saw it. "It goes without saying, I believe," he wrote, "that if we understood ourselves better, we would damage ourselves less. But the barrier between oneself and one's knowledge of oneself is high indeed. There are so many things one would rather not know!"

As an essayist, arguably the greatest America has ever known, Baldwin is concerned primarily (though not solely) with the lies we tell ourselves as Americans. But as a novelist Baldwin is concerned, as all great novelists are concerned, with the distortions and stories and justifications we tell ourselves as human beings:

> [W]e are frightened, all of us, of these forces within us that perpetually menace our precarious security. Yet the forces are there; we cannot will them away. All we can do is learn to live with them. And we cannot learn this unless we are willing to tell the truth about ourselves, and the truth about us is always at variance with what we wish to be.

Checking oneself for self-delusion is like checking oneself for ticks after a walk in the woods: the process is slow and tedious and must be done again and again and again. It's easier not to do it, to just pull off your socks and take the chance. But if the tick is there (and the tick is always there, which is were this metaphor runs into trouble) the price of not checking is incredibly high.

•

The first lies of childhood are preconscious, formed before language begins to shape consciousness. We hold ourselves the center and purpose of the universe, the sun around which everyone else revolves. If we are lucky this lie is broken gently, by loving parents who teach us that while we are the temporary focus of their attention, we are not, in fact, the rising and the setting of the sun. If we are not lucky this lie is broken harshly, by parents who do not love us, or do not love us sufficiently and thus spur the heart-cracking realization that the world was not, in fact, built for us. If we are extremely unlucky this lie is never broken; we grow up and become jerks.

The lies of adolescence and young adulthood are formative and legion. Here is where we either begin the journey towards consciousness or retreat into a lifetime of waking sleep. The lies of young adulthood circle issues of identity and agency and meaning. *Where do I belong in the scheme of things? Why do I have, or not have, the things I have or do not have? How much of what I've been taught is true? What do I deserve from this world? What am I obligated to give?* We answer these questions, and if we lie we set the foundation for bigger, more desperate lies. We pass from innocence into self-delusion, from the world of not knowing to the world of refusing to know.

The journey is slow, indirect, meandering; only the disordered and the downright devilish step boldly from the truth. More often, wrote the Danish philosopher Søren Kierkegaard, we just sit and wait a minute. *I was wrong to hit her.* Well, wait a minute. *This situation is not the fault of the person/group I'm blaming.* Well, wait a minute. *That politician is lying through his teeth.* Well, wait a minute. Then wait a minute more and then a minute more. "...the lower nature's power lies in stretching things out," wrote Kierkegaard.[2] What we know to be true flies unsuspectingly into the Venus flytrap of what we want to believe.

The truth is, the great majority of us live largely lying to ourselves: about ourselves, about our society, about life. *My drinking is fine. Every couple fights like this. I am self-made and self-created. My behavior does not endanger others. He's just afraid of commitment. The divorce was all her fault. Children are resilient. Everything happens for a reason. People get what they deserve. My group is right and yours is wrong. What they say about those people is true. What they say justifies. The moral arc bends. Karma is real. Justice is real. God is real. God does not exist. I know any of this for sure.*

Here are some of the self-deceptions I have identified from my own life, beginning in childhood. This is, of course, a partial list:

- I'm not abandoning my family, I'm saving myself.
- I can make this relationship work if I try hard enough.
- I am more misunderstood than the average person.
- I share no responsibility for my woes.
- I am angry but my anger is righteous and thereby justified.
- I don't hurt others, others hurt me.
- I'm not really going to die.

These seven sentences share a common theme and a common word: *I*. This both is and is not egotistical, in the sense that all human beings are egocentric and all writing is egotistical (as Didion also knew)[3] and yet, if that writing is worthwhile, endeavors to point to something true beyond itself. In this case what the list reveals is that it has been easier for me to lie to myself about myself than to lie to myself about America.

This, it turns out, has been a saving grace.

An example: every year in class I ask the students if they know what important historical event took place on December 6th? They never do, being, for the most part, utterly unfamiliar with the day the thirteenth amendment was ratified, thus abolishing slavery in the United States (with the exception of those convicted of a crime, a not-insignificant clause). I then ask the students whether the country might be different if, say, Abolition Day was a federal holiday. I point out that holidays, like literature, are a people's story of themselves. America's story of itself begins with Columbus (Columbus Day), progresses through the Pilgrims (Thanksgiving) to independence from England (July 4th). It acknowledges some presidents (Washington's Birthday/President's Day) and the Christian nature of the land (Christmas) and the wars we have fought to maintain our way of life (Veteran's Day, Memorial Day) and even the American labor movement (Labor Day). After fierce resistance but fiercer insistence it acknowledges the Civil Rights Movement (MLK Day), but not much more. Nowhere in that story is slavery acknowledged. Nowhere is the foundational truth of this country admitted and revealed.

I ask the students how the nation might be different if Abolition Day were a federal holiday. The students, in their youthful cynicism, say it would make no difference at all, that some people would dismiss it as just a "holiday for Black people" (true) and that no one really takes seriously the holidays we already have (sort of true).

Thus the hegemony both directly and indirectly reinforces itself.

Without doubt I internalized a degree of white supremacy when I was young, wanting green (but not blue) eyes and
long, straight (but not blonde) hair. I thought myself ugly not
because I was Black but because I was dark and fat and short-
haired, which almost, but not quite, amounts to the same thing.
That much of the hegemony I internalized but this much I did
not: by second grade I knew I was smart. By sixth grade I knew
I was as smart or smarter than any boy or girl, white, Black or
otherwise, in my class. Or, since I was in the "advanced class,"
in the school.

Such knowledge creates a kind of cognitive dissonance, a
state of mental tension, which can only be resolved by moderat-
ing one of two conflicting beliefs. "If white people are superior
then Black people must be inferior" is a conditional statement.
I was Black and I was not inferior, therefore the hypothesis did
not stand. And if that central and dominating hypothesis was
untrue then maybe so were others. The hegemony cracked. By
the time *Roots* reached out and slapped America awake (if only
temporarily, as it turned out) I'd already been stirring. I was
thirteen or fourteen and I didn't know what was true but I was
fairly certain the things I was being told were often lies.[4]

Yet clearly *they* believed them. I could see very plainly that
they did.

Didion traces the end of her self-delusion to a loss of innocence, and that loss of innocence to not being elected to Phi Beta
Kappa despite not having the grades. "I lost the conviction that
lights would always turn green for me, the pleasant certainty
that those rather passive virtues which had won me approval as
a child automatically guaranteed me not only Phi Beta Kappa

105

keys but happiness, honor, and the love of a good man (prefera-
bly a cross between Humphrey Bogart in *Casablanca* and one of
the Murchisons in a proxy fight); lost a certain touching faith in
the totem power of good manners, clean hair, and proven com-
petence on the Stanford-Binet scale."

There is a word missing here, a word which highlights that
most passive of all virtues in which many Americans place their
faith. That word, of course, is whiteness. Everyone I know, work
with and/or love is, as far as I can determine, gently or not-so-
gently kidding themselves about something, myself included. But
in sheer, lingering naiveté, in what Baldwin called willful innocence about human nature, about American history, about the
forces shaping our society, about the true nature of the schools
their children attend and the neighborhoods in which they live
and the criminal justice system which they lightly encounter or
largely avoid, about their own, direct and entangled role in all of
this—the white folks win going away. How many times in my
life have I expressed some basic fact (Boston is segregated, public
schools are segregated, policing is not even, government policies
built the white middle class and denied Black access) and been
greeted with shock or disbelief (or denial) by an educated white
person? Once a guy I knew insisted America was rich because
people here work harder than anyone else in the world. When I
pointed out that even among developed countries the US doesn't
crack the top ten in terms of weekly hours worked,[5] and that
none of that compares to the hours the average woman in many
developing countries work (walking three miles a day just to find
water), he was stunned. Which is not to say he changed his mind.

In his great essay "Stranger in the Village," Baldwin wrote:

I do not think . . . that it is too much to suggest that the American vision of the world—which allows so little reality, generally speaking, for any of the darker forces in human life, which tends until today to paint moral issues in glaring black and white—owes a great deal to the battle waged by Americans to maintain between themselves and black men a human separation which could not be bridged. It is only now beginning to be borne in on us—very faintly, it must be admitted, very slowly, and very much against our will—that this vision of the world is dangerously inaccurate, and perfectly useless. For it protects our moral high-mindedness at the terrible expense of weakening our grasp of reality. People who shut their eyes to reality simply invite their own destruction, and anyone who insists on remaining in a state of innocence long after that innocence is dead turns himself into a monster.

Because my investment in whiteness was, luckily, minimal, it was easier for me to see the glaring streak of dirt on the hallway wall. Once seen the dirt cannot be unseen. Nor, if you're awake, can you help looking for dirt on other walls.

•

I am not a romantic. I looked up the meaning of the word once, after someone (a date) accused me of being negative for saying that although I hoped to find someone with whom to spend the rest of my life, there was no guarantee that I would. My date was horrified. He himself belonged to the cult of positive thinking: to even acknowledge the possibility that not every pot would find its lid was heresy. He thought me pessimistic and bitter. I thought him self-delusional and dangerous. (There's a difference between hoping the lights will always turn green for us and believing the universe wills them to do so. We have witnessed the actions of innumerable white men[6] when this belief turns out to be untrue.) Needless to say, it didn't work out.

The word *romance* comes to us from the old French word *romanz* and before that from the Latin *Romanicus,* meaning: "Of the Romans." Originally the word referred to stories told in the vernacular languages: French, Italian, Romanian, Spanish, etc. Serious literature—tracts about philosophy or religion or the nature of man—was written in Latin. Tales about knights and quests and chivalries—frivolous stuff—was thought better suited to the romance languages.

From the OED: *Characterized or marked by, or invested with, a sense of romance (<u>romance n. 5a</u>); arising from, suggestive of, or appealing to, an idealized, fantastic, or sentimental view of life or reality; atmospheric, evocative, glamorous.*

People can be romantic about many things: animals, sports heroes, Beyoncé. But most self-declared romantics are idealistic, fantastical and sentimental about one thing above all: Eros. More than once during my post-divorce dating I met a man who claimed either love-at-first-sight or shortly thereafter, who talked about soul mates and fate and effortless, everlasting bliss. This was sometimes a ploy for sex but not always; more men than I imagined (more men than women, I think) sincerely believe in the fairytale. To express skepticism about such gushing, early declarations or even a simple desire to slow things down usually resulted in being accused of being afraid of my own feelings, or, simply of being negative. "With an attitude like that, you'll never find love," one guy told me. "You're such a pessimist." (In the land of magical thinking, delusion is realism and any attempt at realism is considered being a pessimist. Go figure).

I've never wanted to be a romantic, and yet if there is one area in my life that has shown itself most susceptible to self-delusion it is romance. More than once I told myself someone loved me, or might love me, who clearly did not and would not. More than once I told myself I loved someone unworthy of that love. More than once I tried to turn a frog into a prince. No one is immune.

What most helped wake me from my delusions involving romantic love, I believe, was motherhood. Or rather, what helped me most was the sheer lack of illusions I fortunately carried about that type of love. Even as I peed on that first little stick I did so with zero beliefs about the inherent nature of it all. Other women assured me it was "natural," that maternal instincts belonged to everyone and were thus certain to kick in for me. This is so self-evidently ridiculous I was astonished people could believe it, astonished and not a little terrified. I'd spent the two years before becoming pregnant with my daughter covering the child welfare system in New York City, which was sufficient to refute this mythology. If it weren't, three or four decades of observing the myriad, quotidian acts of violence (emotional, physical, sexual) committed against children by those who professed to love them, would have done the trick. If loving children was instinctive, a significant portion of the human population had somehow lost the instinct. How could I be sure I was not among the damned?

I didn't know what I didn't know, but I knew that I didn't know everything—or possibly anything— about loving a small and defenseless human being (as opposed to simply caretaking one: I had enough experience with other people's children to know something about that). I knew I needed to learn the art of loving my children, and to keep learning it.

Gradually, it occurred to me that if loving my children was profound but not magical, instinctual, perhaps, but not innate, powerful but not mysterious, that loving my children was, in fact, both a gift and an art that needed to be learned (and also needed to be earned), then loving anyone was much the same. Motherhood rid me of both my conscious and unconscious fantasies (glowing and self-abusing) and, in so doing, opened a space for real love to step in.

The fact that real love actually did, is probably just luck. I don't want to delude myself about that.

The Upside to Loving a Sociopath

It is a truth universally acknowledged that the sociopath is best avoided, especially insofar as one values one's sweet and tender heart. The sociopath lies. He cheats without compunction, manipulates without remorse or regret. The sociopath uses and misuses and abandons, and feels justified in doing so: the devil will not be shamed. No sensible person desires to fall in love with a sociopath, just as no sensible person desires to contract herpes under the skin. It happens. It happens even to the best of us, and (like herpes) to more people than you believe. Despite one's best intentions one may find one has handed over one's heart to a person incapable of cherishing it or even treating it with dignity, but perfectly capable of using it to wipe his feet. What then, Gentle Reader? What then?

Contrary to most essays on the subject, this treatise seeks to reassure the reader that loving a sociopath does not have to be all gloom and doom! There are benefits, real and vital benefits, to be gained from giving one's heart to a merciless monster, gifts to be received. Speaking from personal experience this writer can offer proof that loving a sociopath can be no worse than say, falling from a high place and shattering one's arm. Will it be painful? Most certainly. Yet barring unforeseen circumstances such as gangrene or the production of offspring, the pain will diminish and the bone will mend stronger at the broken places, as Hemingway said.

•

A definition: the DSM-5 places both psychopaths and sociopaths in the category of antisocial personality disorder. A person with antisocial personality disorder has three or more of the following traits:

- He regularly breaks or flouts the law.
- She constantly lies and deceives others.
- He is impulsive, does not like to plan ahead.
- She can be prone to fighting and aggressiveness.
- He has little regard for the safety or well-being of others.
- She is irresponsible and/or can't meet financial obligations.
- He does not feel remorse or guilt.

Psychopaths are born, sociopaths are made, say psychiatrists. Roughly three percent of the U.S. population are one or the other, with men more likely than women to be both. Psychopaths are shrewder, more manipulative and charming, more likely to lead a semblance of a normal life. Sociopaths are more likely to be erratic, rage-prone and reckless, more likely to commit crimes of passion than dispassionate crime. Neither one cares about your heart.

Not all sociopaths/psychopaths are violent, Hollywood

fantasies to the contrary. Chances are your sociopath will wound only your one, precious heart, but one must be careful. If your sociopath has violent tendencies this brief missive is not for you. Seek qualified guidance. Be safe and get help.

Those of us who must tangle with nonviolent sociopaths will focus on the benefits.

•

Upside #1: *At least you're dating.*

I did not date during the separation from my husband, or for awhile after the divorce. Dating was not on the radar, only survival and picking up.

Abstaining from an intimate relationship is like abstaining from food for a period: after the first week or so you don't even feel hungry anymore. By the time The Poet came along I was so deep into solitude all I saw at first glance was the size of his ears and the ticking of the clock showing how long before I slip out of the theater and go home. Then he read a poem about his father and the hunger pains came roaring back. Things did not work out with The Poet. All loving him did was to make my heart hungry again.

Hungry hearts are like chum in the water to the Sociopath.

I met the sociopath online. Online dating websites, even respectable ones, are a common arena for encountering the sociopath, but no more so than the pickup lane of your child's school or the United States senate or the conference room at work. Like spiders and motorcycles, sociopaths are everywhere: sometimes you see them, sometimes you don't.

Once launched, I took to online dating rather like a bankrupt mathematician plays the lottery: you know precisely the odds against winning, but what else are you going to do? At first it was fun, if by fun you mean excruciating and humiliating. The endless supply of handsome and available men who turn out to be neither. The thrill of a first meeting that sours almost immediately into dread. The excitement of possibility that quickly becomes the assurance of nothing even remotely feasible coming from such an endeavor. You can't go on. You must go on. You go on.

You meet all kinds: the Eager Beaver, the Sad Sack, the Bitter Woman-Hater. The Aging Player and the Playing With His Age (*lying). The Emotionally Still-Married and the Legally-So (For "the kids." Or the house or the taxes or the sex). The Juvenile. The Baffled and the Oblivious.

This last type of man, surprisingly plentiful, is wounded and surprised to find himself divorced. He liked being married, thought everything was going great. Had a nice house and well-tended children. Occasional if not plentiful sex. Season tickets to the Patriots. One such man told me: "I was happily married for twenty-two years. Unfortunately it turned out my wife was happily married for only about eight or nine."

"You didn't notice?" I asked, astonished.

"I was busy."

"For a decade?"

He shrugged.

These guys will either prove as slippery as eels or as clingy as tics. They will be ten to twenty years older than yourself because a younger woman is what they believe they deserve and the ones your own age will believe the same. They, most of them, will not be in shape.

After two or four or six years of this you walk into a bar expecting yet another dead-end meeting, already planning to cut out gracefully and be home in time for Jeopardy and there sits the Sociopath. He is reasonably tall, reasonably funny, good-looking in a boyish sort of way (hint, hint). He reeks of sexuality, which most of the men you have been meeting do not. He is a public school teacher in the city, which you misinterpret to mean he cares about the liberating power of education. You are, of course, utterly wrong.

Have you ever been hungry? I mean desperately hungry: your mouth bitter with acid, your lips dry and crackly, your stomach twisting in agony? In the human brain, emotional impulses originate in the amygdala, an almond-shaped structure that triggers the physiological reactions connected to emotions. These physiological reactions include the release of certain neurochemicals—chemicals that are also released when an event or image is recalled.

What this means is that it's not just "in your mind"—it's in your brain. And your bloodstream and your arteries and your heart.

What happened inside when first I met the Sociopath? Certainly there was sexual desire, but that was not the only thing. Almost instantly I developed a craving for the Sociopath that went beyond anything I had ever felt. In retrospect it's easy to see this was a craving not simply or even primarily for sex but for something equally primal, something higher in tier in Maslow's contested pyramid, something much, much harder to get: Love. Approval. Being chosen. Which is connected to security. Which is one step down (meaning one step more fundamental) in our needs.

Here's the pop psychology version, dear Reader, to save us both a little time:

If, despite the best efforts of one parent and the utter indifference of another, a person never felt loved as a child, that person may grow seeking that love among people incapable of giving it, thereby subconsciously replicating his/her experience over and over again.

Ain't that some stuff?

●

Upside #2: *The sex will be good.*

They say love is mysterious. Then again, they say a lot of stupid things. Love is no more mysterious, no more inexplicable than schizophrenia. We do not know all there is to know about schizophrenia: who gets it or what, precisely it does to the brain or why. We don't know these things about schizophrenia but just because we don't know these things doesn't mean these things are *unknowable*. Even as I write this sentence some scientist somewhere is hard at work, cracking the code of this human phenomenon, powering ahead in the belief that comprehension is out there, just beyond our grasp. "Love is mysterious" they say. Just like they used to say about the moon.

I walked into that bar and sat down next to the Sociopath and my pheromones leapt up to crash against his like two roosters loosed into a pit. That's not mysterious: that's some serious chemical/biological reaction taking place, my animal brain picking up some companionable, matable scent.

An hour later I left the restaurant, floating on clouds that only scudded a little when a text arrived, asking that I meet him at his house.

Um, we just met.

So?

A male friend once told me that straight men place every woman they meet immediately into one of three categories: 1) Potential Fuck Buddy, 2) Potential Girlfriend, 3) Invisible. "Once you've been placed in the first category, it's rare to get out," he said. Now if a man I'd just met but to whom I was *not* violently, subconsciously attracted texted me on the way home from our first meeting and invited me to his house, I'd drop him like a slug-covered piece of wood. No interest in being placed in box number one, thanks very much.

But for some reason I didn't do that with the Sociopath.

Even if I did that kind of thing, which I don't, my children are home. I left them for an hour but I can't leave them longer.

Come on.

Maybe some other time. ;)

I actually used an emoticon. If that didn't slap me out of my stupor nothing was going to do so.

Here's some backstory: before the Sociopath came a season of abstinence. And before that, the Rain Main. The Rain Man was tall and handsome and well-intentioned, and as stunted as drought-stricken corn. Emotionally, I mean. When I asked, flirtatiously, what had drawn him to my online profile he said, "You fit my parameters." When I said that I'd taken down my profile because I noticed he'd taken down his he said, "I was getting too many emails. I've optimized my profile to receive 4.3 messages a day but in doing so it was taking up too much time." Not precisely the "why go out for hamburger" line I'd hoped to hear.

The first time we had sex, he thanked me. "Dude," I said. "I didn't take your suit to the cleaners. *We* had sex. Do not thank me."

What the Rain Man's gratitude helped to confirm was the fundamental male ignorance of female sexuality, an ignorance so profound as to be nearly comical. For most men, female sexuality is like mountaineering: there are a hundred-and-one ways to get things disastrously wrong. One of these ways is engage in the popular belief that women dislike sex.

What women disfavor, kind sirs, is not sex itself but being pressured, hounded or forced into having said activity. Say that you enjoy burritos. Imagine that some stranger accosted you on the street and forced one down your throat. Or that your own loving partner hounded you to have one every time you crawled exhausted into bed. You might reasonably object, and your objection would be to the coercion, not the burrito, *n'est-ce pas?*

The Rain Man believed, as do many other men, that women "gift" men sex primarily or even solely in exchange for what they *really* desire: money, babies, love. This may be true for some women some of the time but it is true of some women none of the time and all women neither.

"Then why do so many women, women in relationships, avoid sex?" the Rain Man asked me.

"Maybe because so many men suck at it?"

He seemed dubious. Or perhaps simply taken aback.

"Consider," I suggested, "Brussels sprouts. I always thought I hated Brussels sprouts, but then I had some that had been roasted with garlic and salt instead of boiled into a disgusting mush. Now I love Brussels sprouts. I cannot get enough."

The Rain Man was not roasted Brussels sprouts but I refrained from so saying. Protecting a man's ego is one thing women are certainly taught.

Which leads us back to the Sociopath. During our time together (so to speak) those around often inquired as to why, precisely, I remained with him. My friends asked. *His* friends asked. ("You guys seem an unlikely couple," one of his friends said, delicately. "He's always been selfish," said another bud.) A sweet young bartender (who had probably seen him in the bar with a dozen women) asked once, half-joking. Another time, during a painful, off-again period, a friend and I were at a bar when she got into conversation with two sweet French guys we thought were gay (turns out only one of them was; the other was married to a woman). Somehow the Sociopath's name came up and it turned out the married French guy knew him. He gave me a sorrowful French look and shook his perfect head.

"He is a lost soul, beyond salvation,," said Frenchie. "Trust me, you are better off."

When strange French men at bars warn you away like some kind of Greek chorus, you know that things have gotten bad.

Even the Sociopath himself, in brief, fleeting moments of humanity, would sometimes ask. One time we drove our separate cars back to his house from the place where we'd been having a drink. I arrived first. It was dark but I stood in the glow from the streetlamp with my little red hat on and when he pulled up in his car and climbed out he stopped mid-walk and looked at me:

"Why are you here?"

"You said to come over."

"No, I mean what are *you* doing *here?*"

I shrugged. The answer was large and complicated and also small and noisome and the last thing I wanted to think about at that moment. The answer might force me to stop being there.

He had some virtues. He was funny in a kind of juvenile way I found refreshing after days in tedious, self-important academia. He was a teacher, and I admire teachers. He was not afraid of Black people as so many white people are. He thought Black women sexy and beautiful and desirable, which even a lot of Black men in Boston do not. He was not afraid of, or intimidated by, me.

These things were true but mostly the reason was psycho-sexual, meaning the physical attraction was real and powerful, but not as powerful as the subconscious yearning to win what could never be won. Of course, it's only easy to see that last part now.

For three dates I resisted his invitations to his house. I say "dates" but really I mean meetings: he never asked me out on an actual date. Instead he would text me at five-thirty or six o'clock after he was done with work and ask if I wanted to meet somewhere for a drink, which he would not buy. We would meet and talk and flirt and laugh and if I was hungry I would buy myself something to eat.

"You're hot," he would say and I would laugh because it was so basic. And so appealing. The Rain Man had told me how "attractive" I was. I gently explained that being called attractive does not spin a girl's heart. He insisted it was a high-level compliment, that it meant men were attracted to me. I pointed out that men have been known to be attracted to farm animals. Saying someone is attractive is like saying the Grand Canyon is nice.

The Sociopath told me I was hot and I responded with hotness and although everything outside of his bedroom was cold-hearted and broken, everything inside of it was hot.

Was the sex good because he was a sociopath? I can't say; my experience with sociopaths has been, thankfully, limited. Still, it seems likely the Sociopath's sociopathy (sociopathology?) played some not insignificant role in his skillfulness. A big part of being good at sex is being able to step out from beneath the weight of ego and societal dictates and expectations, to shed religious baggage and cultural myths, to set aside inhibitions and self-consciousness. Turns out it's a lot easier to be *un*-self-conscious if one has no self. Or no consciousness.

•

Upside #3: *You'll realize just how much shit you are willing to tolerate.*

And so we come to the crux of it, to the required Litany of

Complaints in which I detail all the shoddy treatment. When I tell you, Dear Reader, how he'd pursue me with a passion, calling and texting until I relented, then disappear. How he mimicked a relationship, claiming my weekends, taking me to his high school reunion, introducing me to his childhood friends—then pulled out the rug. (And then did it all over again). How he liked to nip at my self-confidence, mocking my drum-playing, "joking" about my job. How he never bothered to ask about my children or my writing or my family or my life. How his friends warned me away from him. How the mother of his child hated him. Also the principals of the schools in which he taught (and from which he was inevitably "released" after a year or two).

"He's not very kind to you," said a friend after a dinner party at which he had relentlessly "teased" me about my cooking, my drum-playing, my life. "He's not very kind to you," was pretty much the kindest thing any of my friends had to say about The Sociopath, which is perhaps why it actually landed.

"You're right," I told my friend. "He is not very kind at all."

•

Upside #4: *You will discover your own inner sociopath.*

My exit began on Good Friday. For weeks I'd been trying to wrench myself from the situation, knowing it was headed no place good. But here it was Friday and I was tired and depleted and so lonely I could chew off an arm. All of my friends were busy. So when he texted to see if I was free for a drink, I said yes.

We met, we talked, we flirted. He pulled my chair closer, touched my hair, otherwise mimicked the actions of a human being. When a blousy red-haired chick stopped to say hello he chatted for a second, then turned back to me. I was happy. I should have known.

One of the friends I'd called earlier called back to see if I could meet her somewhere. She had no transportation and needed someone to talk to. I invited the Sociopath along but he declined, saying my friend disliked him. Which she did. Then he asked what I was doing afterwards. Said he'd be home in an hour or so.

"I'll come by," I said.

"Okay. But if you text me and I don't respond because I'm sleeping or something, don't get upset."

"Okay," I said, not really taking this in.

An hour or so later I texted to say that I was finishing up with my girlfriend and would stop by. No response.

At this point I must confess that this kind of thing had happened before, a few months prior. The same pattern: a texted invitation to meet. Me, responding that I was at work at the moment but suggesting we meet later. A vague agreement on his part, followed by silence when I later reach out to him. A sinking feeling and a drive, despite knowing better, to his house. A woman in the living room.

Yes, it had happened before and I was ashamed to admit it then and I am ashamed to admit it now. How many times does someone have to kick you in the heart before you run?

Which explains why this time I am not so much shocked as wounded and furious. Furious at him and furious, furious at myself.

I drove to his house. The lights were on and the music was

going. He opened the door to my ring, told me to go home, then shut it in my face. I leaned on the doorbell for a few minutes, meaning to drag him out, wanting only to make him look into my face and see the pain he had caused. It felt critical that he be forced to see the pain.

When he didn't open the door I walked toward the back of the house, toward the kitchen. I could see through the slats in the kitchen door blinds that they were standing there. I knocked. The woman urged him to open the door, then did it herself. She was red-haired and blousy and utterly smashed, and I recognized her from the restaurant where we were earlier. The woman who'd stopped to say hello to him.

She stationed herself dizzily in the doorway, wanting to talk earnestly to me, sister to sister. "Listen, listen, listen," she slurred. "It's not sexual. I just broke up with this guy and we're talking, is all."

"You poor thing," I said, because she was not only wasted but an idiot. But my beef was not with her; I stepped around. He leaned against the kitchen sink, wine glass in hand.

"What is wrong with you?" I asked, and I'm not so much angry anymore as desperate, desperate to understand. Even now, at what is clearly the end I felt an urgent need for an explanation. More than anything I wanted to understand how people could be so brutally selfish, so casually and astonishingly unkind.

"Are you some kind of sociopath?" I asked him. The word arrived out of nowhere, a handle to grasp. "Is that why you're like this? Do you not think that other people have feelings? Are you crazy? Are you sick?"

All he did was smirk.

Behind me the woman fumbled for a cigarette. "I'm going to need a ride home in about ten minutes," she slurred.

I drove home feeling despondent and debased, pretty sure I'd end up sobbing on the kitchen floor the way I had so many nights, not necessarily over this guy but over the aching wound of loneliness, over what felt—rightly or wrongly—like the chronic and overwhelming absence of love in my life. "What difference does it make if what scared you is real or not?" wrote Toni Morrison. At home I turned on the kitchen light and got a glass of water, tears sloshing down my face.

Then I saw the scissors.

They were long and sharp and pointed and what was strange was that I had stumbled across them in a drawer just that morning, after months of not knowing where they were. I had taken them out to cut paper for a package I was mailing.

I could say I'd had a glass of wine. I could say I moved in a blind fury, a waking dream. I could say I was too dazed with pain and fear, the fear of a four-year-old girl from whom love is being removed, to fully realize what I was doing. Some of that would be true but none of it would be completely true so maybe none of it is relevant. I knew what I was doing. I knew, though if I had stopped to think I probably would not have proceeded.

I made sure not to stop to think.

The whole thing took maybe ten minutes. I drove back to his house, parked in the supermarket parking lot a block away. I walked casually to the front of his house, slowing to let a woman walking on the opposite side clear the area. At his car I kneeled, stabbed, removed. The hiss of air from his back tire was like the breaking of a fever, like being shaken awake from a very bad dream. I pocketed my scissors and rose.

I woke the next morning horrified and deeply ashamed of my actions, and that eventually I made ethical and financial amends. That the Sociopath never acknowledged or apologized for his behavior only proves his sociopathology. That I descended to his level proves one never knows what one is capable of until one does.

It's good to learn these things. That's how you decide never to do them again.

●

Upside #5: *You realize it's not about you.*

I once met a man, a handsome man, a tall and sexy man, a man to whom I was drawn except for one unfortunate fact: he was still involved with his ex-wife. By *involved* I don't mean sexually or legally, but emotionally: he hated her. A lot. This tall and sexy man spent twenty minutes of our one and only meeting discussing her and her betrayals, twenty minutes during which I journeyed from disappointment to astonishment to boredom to sympathy, because this man was not the first duped or dumped human being hiding his hurt beneath a mountain of bitterness whom I had met and because as the hour wore on and the chance of a second date crumbled into dust beneath the weight of his surprised and angry woundedness it became increasingly clear he could not move on from his pain because he failed to grasp one simple and salient fact: everyone gets one sociopath.

This is a fundamental fact of life, a law of the universe, and the moment you embrace it is the moment you are free. Everyone gets at least one sociopath, one asshole, one hurtful and narcissistic jerk who barges or stumbles or falls into their life and causes pain. The boyfriend who slept with your roommate and tried to gaslight his way out of the truth. The cheating wife who lied to the judge. The disapproving partner who tried to keep you under his or her thumb.

Everyone gets one sociopath just like everybody gets a cold sometimes or trips over a ragged or icy sidewalk or gets into an accident while tootling along in his or her car. These things can be terrible, of course—painful and damaging and even life-threatening, but mostly they aren't. Mostly, thankfully, they are nuisances. Mostly we deal with them without the added psychic misery of believing ourselves to have been somehow uniquely targeted, uniquely infected, uniquely hurt. The greatest upside of loving a sociopath is surviving him. If you can do that without bitterness but with gratitude and insight, it was worth the adventure.

Next time, though: wash your hands.

A Case for the Selective, Targeted, Nonviolent Act of Revenge

By rough calculation, I have been mistreated, disrespected, or generally screwed-over or wronged three hundred and fifty-nine times in my life. That's only a guesstimate, of course. I have not been keeping track.

To arrive at the number I reviewed the year just past and recalled five or six such incidents. Most were petty and some grievous and some were in-between. Multiply five by my age, subtract some for the toddler years (because toddlerhood is mostly about dishing out disrespect), double-down for adolescence and toss in some extra for the years I spent laboring in the newsroom of the *New York Times*. Voilà: three hundred and fifty-nine instances of physical, emotional, or psychological wounding. Yet only twice have I sought revenge— and only one of those times, already detailed, involved destruction of property.

Honestly, I think that's pretty good.

•

The first boy to break my heart was the first one to whom I gave it. This is pretty standard; if your teen romance ended not in tears and mournful mixtapes, you probably did it wrong.

His name was Tony and he was tall and lanky and white, after a fashion. I was tall and shapely and Black, after a fashion. We met at boarding school in New Hampshire, a strange and chilly place, surreal for both of us. He took me for pizza, made me mixtapes, introduced me to the Sugar Hill Gang, gave me a dozen red roses for Valentine's Day. I took it all, wary and ecstatic. No male human being save my brother had ever really loved me before, but Geoff's affection meant such loving was possible. Part of me prayed it would last forever. Part of me knew it would not.

I don't remember the precise reason it fell apart. Maybe because I wouldn't sleep with him or maybe he got bored or maybe I was a confused and contradictory mess. Maybe he was young and confused himself, finding his way in a bifurcated world: white skin, Black stepfather, child of Harlem and fancy boarding school. I don't even remember how he told me, what words he used, whether we stood together in the snow outside my dorm or the pain sliced over the phone. All I remember is that it hurt deeply for awhile and then less so, and that he moved on to someone else before getting into trouble and being expelled from school.

What lessons we take from life depend so much on the classroom to which we've been assigned. By the time I landed in boarding school I was pretty sure I was too much to be loved: too tall, too fat, too Black. There are reasons for this—absent father, mother herself unloved and overwhelmed, an omnipresent cultural representation of Blackness as ugliness—but in general people did the best they could with the tools they had at the time and so this is not about assigning blame. The point is simply that I entered the world of romantic love not believing myself worthy, and so what I took from that first heartbreak was confirmation. Geoff was the first boy to break my heart but it never occurred to me to seek revenge against him. This was the right impulse but the reason behind it, strangely, was wrong.

Not everyone who breaks your heart is a monster. Not everyone who wounds you deserves to be wounded in return. Geoff was not and did not but those are not the reasons I failed to consider revenge. I sought no revenge against Geoff because his wounding of me seemed not only expected but justifiable: the sure and natural course of things. Geoff hurt me but I was never angry at his hurting, not even a little. It was my own damn fault for losing his love.

•

It's hard to find anyone willing to say a good, public word about revenge. Our greatest writers almost universally advocate forgiveness. In *Paradise Lost*, Milton warned, "Revenge, at first though sweet, Bitter ere long back on itself recoils." Francis Bacon called revenge a "a kind of wild justice, which the more man's nature runs to, the more ought law to weed it out." Shakespeare gave us Shylock and Iago, neither one meant as appealing. Melville made Ahab a foaming nut. Not the world's major religions, which either caution against revenge or outright forbid it. Sorta. "Don't take vengeance and don't bear a grudge against the members of your nation; love your neighbor as yourself," reads Leviticus 19:18. Yet, the Old Testament also clearly advocates the *lex talionis*—the law of retaliation—a

Babylonian principle taken up by the Romans which advocates that the punishment should fit the crime, precisely. That means an eye for an eye, and only one eye. You don't have to forgive and forget, but you don't get to blind the guy.

In some books of the Bible, God makes clear that fixing people good is His job: "Vengeance is mine, I will repay, saith the Lord." But at other times God gives man permission to take revenge: after the Midianites behaved badly God gave Moses the green light. Moses not only sent his army to wipe out the male Midianites, but when the soldiers returned with captives he scolded them. "Have you allowed all the women to live? They were the ones who followed Balaam's advice and enticed the Israelites to be unfaithful . . . kill all the boys. And kill every woman who has slept with a man, but save for yourselves every girl who has never slept with a man."

Whoa.

In the New Testament, Jesus moves his followers beyond this idea of metered justice, urging them toward a more radical love. Do not resist an evil person, Jesus says. Turn the other cheek, love your enemy, pray for those who persecute you. Paul reiterates the teachings of Jesus, but Paul, being Paul, cannot help but do so with a sting: "If your enemy is hungry, feed him; if he is thirsty, give him something to drink. In doing this, you will heap burning coals on his head."

Islam does not require its followers to turn the other cheek but the Holy Qur'an makes it clear that forgiveness is the higher path. Buddhism concurs. "We should not seek revenge on those who have committed crimes against us, or reply to their crimes with other crimes," writes the Dalai Lama. "We should reflect that by the law of karma, they are in danger of lowly and miserable lives to come, and that our duty to them, as to every being, is to help them to rise towards Nirvana, rather than let them sink to lower levels of rebirth."

All of which is to say that most of what religion has to say is this: leave it to God. Leave it for Allah, for Jehovah, to karma to settle accounts. Leave it to God because God, unlike man, can be counted upon not to act from impure motives. Also, God will make whatever you've got planned look like a garden party. Ask Pharaoh. He knows.

Philosophers and social scientists and legal experts are more conflicted on the subject, as philosophers and social scientists and legal experts will tend to be. The desire for revenge is natural but immoral; the desire for revenge is human and empowering. Some have tried to clear the waters by parsing the difference between punishment and revenge. The German philosopher Eugen Dühring argued that the very concept of injustice stems from the natural feeling of resentment we have against those who have wronged us, and thus even the most impersonal punishment is a form of revenge.

Nietzsche, who considered the matter deeply (and, it must be said, misogynistically) suggested that people who insisted that all revenge stemmed from one single idea or motivation were, essentially, idiots: "As if all words were not pockets, into which this or that or several things have been stuffed at once! So revenge is now one thing, now another, and sometimes more composite." Revenge, wrote Nietzsche, can be either self-preservation (striking out at a person to prevent further hurt) or readjustment (a usually futile attempt to settle scores). Futile because revenge will not return whatever was destroyed by the action of the offender—unless that thing was honor. Limbs and loved ones and burned houses cannot be reclaimed if taken, but honor can. An intentional attack proves the attacker is not afraid of us. Revenge proves we are not afraid of him. Thus balance is restored.

In such case, writes Nietzsche, a person will forgo revenge for only three reasons:

- He loves the offender.
- He finds the offender beneath his contempt and bother.
- He kinda despises himself. "Depending on whether he projects himself strongly or weakly into the soul of his opponent and the spectators, his revenge will be more embittered or tamer; if he lacks this type of imagination entirely, he will not think of revenge at all, for in that case the feeling for 'honor' is not present in him and hence cannot be injured."

In other words, revenge will never occur to the one who lacks the self-esteem to be offended, who views the cruel and casual slogging of her heart as painful but expected, life's little par for the course. Revenge will not occur to the one who suspects she deserves such mistreatment, who believes life grants for her only the attentions of such blatant, unrelenting jerks. "A small revenge is more human than no revenge at all," Nietzsche said.

•

Between Tony and the first rising of my revenge lay some thirty-odd years of relationships, the bulk of which I spent with one very good and decent man. S and I met when I was nineteen and he was twenty. I was a sophomore in college, plowing my way forward to a more secure life. He had dropped out and was working in a restaurant and hanging out with friends, trying to figure out how to restart his life. Turned out I could help with that.

During our time together I graduated and got a job as a reporter and he went back to school and I got another job and he got his degree and I got another job and we moved to Philadelphia and he went to grad school and we got married and I got another job and he finished his PhD and we moved to New York and got a dog and had a child and I wrote a novel and quit my job and had another child and he got a job and we moved to Boston and the marriage came slowly apart. Assigning fault seems ridiculous in retrospect, though fault was assigned at the time, by me to me. The truth is, I'd seen a lot of marriages crumble but only two ways that people dealt with the destruction: self-flagellation or angry unforgiveness. I knew enough to know that unforgiveness was like swallowing poison and waiting for the other person to die, so I went with self-flagellation.

Turns out there is another way.

•

Lawyer Man and I met online. He was tall and dark and handsome, a successful attorney with two red-flag marriages under his belt, which of course I ignored. On our first date Lawyer Man drove forty minutes to meet me, bought me dinner and kissed me in the rain. By date three he was declaring his love. By date five he'd decided my skeptical and disbelieving response was caused by fear and that his job was to knock down my wall of resistance and distrust.

These are some of the things he said to me during that time. I wrote them down, as writers will:

I'll take care of you, if you let me.

Don't let your brain get in the way.

You're my girl. You know you are.

Open your heart to me. Okay you don't have to open it, just don't close it. Don't throw me overboard.

In other words: a romantic. I didn't realize at the time because I didn't know men could be romantics, not outside of novels or absurd movies from Hollywood. Now I know better; the older I get the more I believe that men are the true romantics, the ones clinging hardest and longest to the fantasy of life-changing, unwavering lust/attraction/love. At the time, though, I thought Lawyer Man said all those things because of me. He stood before me, gushing desire and affection and I believed the wellspring of all that effluence to be myself. But really the source was his love of the idea of love. I was just there getting wet.

For ten months he urged me into the deep end of connection, until finally, after a picture-perfect weekend in Montreal, I was immersed. In over my head and loving it and for another week or two we swam together, happy and satisfied. Then, suddenly and without warning, he got out.

In retrospect there were signs. One night at dinner with his friends he nastily mocked something I said. I laughed it off. Or tried. Another night I climbed into bed and curled against him, but instead of wrapping his long arms around me he patted my back like a dog. The next morning he barely kissed me goodbye.

A few days later I opened my email to a lethal little bomb: *it's not working, I need space, it's too hard*, some other shit I don't recall. After the first few lines I stopped reading, halted by adrenalin and a very real feeling of terror, as though someone had reached through the screen and jabbed me in the gut. In a panic I forwarded the email to a friend then deleted it. I called her, sobbing. "Read it, please. Read it and tell me what it means."

This reaction may seem extreme. It seemed extreme to my friend, a stable, competent, matter-of-fact woman whose standard reaction to my repeated cases of heartbreak is, "Well, that just means he's not worthy of you. Sucks all around. Move on." It took me a long time to understand why I could not share such bloodless common sense about heartbreak. It took me a long, long time to understand why I couldn't, as everyone kept so helpfully advising, just shake that shit off.

It's this: There's a reason babies scream when you put them down. There's a reason toddlers, waking to find themselves alone in a car or an unknown room, convulse with terror. When you are a young child and love is taken from you it feels as if you might die because you really might. Without love a child is vulnerable; without care and protection a child cannot survive the brutal world. When you have not been sufficiently loved as a child losing love will always be difficult. Losing love will always feel, at least in the moment, as if you are about to die.

My friend told me what Lawyer Man had really said but all I heard was, *Love is gone. Love is gone because you are unlovable.* Still panicking, I dialed his phone number. He didn't answer. I left a message, asking for a call. Ten minutes later I dialed again, begging now. No response. I dialed and dialed and dialed.

•

It's a dangerous confession for a woman to make, admitting to anger. Angry women are either Medea or Madea, either ruthless or ridiculous, laughable or indiscriminate, dripping in blood. Angry women don't play in Peoria.

Angry men . . . well, that's different; all of American culture roots for the angry (white) man. I used to know a guy, his favorite movie was *Unforgiven*, Clint Eastwood's meditation on violence and the myth of the old west. He saw it twice in the theaters, then bought the video and watched it probably a dozen more times at home. One time I watched it with him, and even though Clint Eastwood generally sets my teeth on edge and it dismayed me to see Morgan Freeman in his usual pseudo-dignified shuck-and-jive I found myself appreciating the film. Beautifully shot, sharply acted violence one might both condemn and cheer. Two hours of moral ambiguity and satisfying bloodlust. Quite the accomplishment.

My friend waited excitedly for his favorite line of dialogue, which comes near the end of the film. Morgan Freeman's character is dead. Another character, the Kid, who had been so eager to earn his manhood by murder, has sickened on the actual violence and departed. Gene Hackman, the villain, lies on the floor, Eastwood's gun at his neck. "I don't deserve to die," he barks, unrepentant.

"Deserving's got nothing to do with it," Eastwood growls, then shoots him in the head. My friend cheered.

Eastwood pockets his cake and eats it too in *Unforgiven*, condemning macho-fueled violence (Eastwood's character was a brutal gunslinger civilized by the love of his saintly wife) while suggesting that sometimes targeted mayhem is the only way of protecting the innocent and setting things right.

In this way the movie sits neatly aside other male revenge fantasies, from *Cape Fear* to *Gladiator*, from *Get Carter* to *Taken*, from *Mad Max* to that mother-of-all revenge films *Death Wish* (one, two, and three). Not to mention *The Godfather*. Pacino, Hoffman, DiCaprio, Gibson, Crowe, Neeson, Washington, Willis—it's hard to name a major male Hollywood star over the last four decades who has not taken up arms in revenge. The plots are yawningly similar: our hero is minding his business when some jerk comes along and screws with him, usually by kidnapping/raping/murdering some woman in his life: his wife, his daughter, even his mother (*Four Brothers*). It doesn't really matter since the woman exists mostly to give our hero an excuse to unleash his inner warrior. Off he goes to wreak vengeance. He's not irrational or deranged, just dangerous. It's a good kind of dangerousness, a sexy kind of menace. A man doing what he must.

Female revenge seekers, on the other hand, are usually

either laughable (*First Wives Club, The Other Woman, 9 to 5*), troubled and unstable (*Columbiana, Brave One*), flat-out crazy (*Fatal Attraction*) or downright monstrous (*Carrie*).[7] What they seek is not so much vengeance as revenge, which is comparatively petty. Whatever violence was done to their hearts or even their bodies was regrettable but really of minor significance.

My favorite line in *Unforgiven* comes midway through the film when the Kid, shaken after committing his first homicide, tries to muster his bravado. "Yeah. Well, I guess they had it coming," he squeaks.

Eastwood, squinting, replies, "We all have it coming, kid."

A wise and thoughtful sentiment, except that in the movie only the bad guys—along with the innocent Black guy, of course, always the Black guy—get what's coming to them. Eastwood wreaks his vengeance and goes quietly back to his pig farm. The Kid, who killed to prove himself a man, rides off into the sunset, redeemed and reclaimed.

•

Listen, shit happens: I get that. People fall out of love, people change their minds and change their hearts. Okay. People decide, after a few short weeks, that you are the love of their life and spend months trying to convince you of that, only to revoke that declaration the minute you give in. Fair enough.

But dumping a person by email? Refusing to pick up the phone and speak to the desperate person on the other end of the line?

I considered getting into my car and driving to Lawyer

Man's house to demand an accounting, but my children and the forty-five minute drive cooled that idea. God watches out for children and fools. Sometimes anyway.

Instead I did what women do when men cruelly and unceremoniously dump them: I cried. I cried, hiding it from the kids as best as possible, gritting my way through otherwise. I lost my appetite, couldn't sleep. I dismissed my friends when they said, "It's his loss," since it was my loss I was worried about. I ricocheted back and forth between anger and abject self-loathing. What was wrong with me? Was I not pretty enough, or smart enough or too smart? Had I caused this with my caution? Was this my fault for not believing soon enough in his love?

For weeks I suffered. Then one morning, as I was reading the newspaper, an idea arrived. I'd just browsed some story about new treatment for sexually-transmitted diseases and the idea just sprung. I opened an email to him, wrote "health issue" in the subject line and left the email blank. Then I hit *send*.

Ten minutes later he telephoned. I let it go to voicemail.

"Hi. It's me. Um, your email came through but it was blank."

He had ghosted me pretty efficiently. But I found the Ouija board.

"Is there something I should know? Give me a call."

I laughed. I mean I laughed: loud and hard and long. I laughed as I had not laughed in weeks and it was wonderful—a revelation, an unburdening. Which was what I needed, because that's what assholes do: they burden you not with their unlove but with their selfish and callous and casual dismissal of your humanity. There's a difference between someone who breaks your heart and a heartbreaker; someone can break a heart with tenderness and consciousness and regret. But a heartbreaker has no regard for the vital human organ upon which he tramples. And a bastard—a monster, a villain, a brute—is even worse. A bastard does not even believe that's a heart beneath his feet. He thinks it is so much mulch, put down to smooth his walk.

For several days he phoned, increasingly worried. Eventually I must have let him off the hook, but the truth is, I can't recall. I don't remember exactly what happened after that because after that email I was done. The spell was broken, my sense of self restored. No longer the victim, I could forget (if not precisely forgive) and move on.

And that's the point.

•

In my heart I know there is really no way to make a case for revenge. In my heart I know that revenge draws a circle of hate and damage, real and imagined, emotional and physical. You hurt me (or I think you did) so I hurt you, so you hurt me again and again until one of us is dead or we're both so broken we wish we were.

The truth is I am not ashamed of my two targeted, non-violent, singular and specific acts of revenge. The victims were inconvenienced but not injured (I eventually gave the Sociopath money for a new tire). I'm not ashamed of my acts of petty revenge because without them I would have gone on as in the past, feeling helpless and victimized, a hapless insect under some asshole's dirty boot. I'm not ashamed of my acts of petty revenge because the painful truth is goodness does not always win in the end and karma is not nearly the bitch we might want her to be. The high road is potholed and lonely and nobody really knows where it leads; the low road gets there fast. People get away with being selfish and mean-spirited. If they didn't, there'd be a lot fewer jerks running around.

I'm not ashamed of my petty acts of revenge, but I'm ashamed of not being ashamed. I really am.

I know how dangerous this is, encouraging even small, nonviolent, singular, and specific acts of revenge. I know where it leads for many people, where it leads for the world, where it could lead for me. An eye for eye leaves the whole world blind, said Gandhi, and we are already lost and stumbling. My small, singular, nonviolent, and specific acts of revenge actually helped me grow into a stronger person more capable of forgiveness, but that's an irony we cannot really afford broad-scale. This is the world I leave behind for my children, a world sufficiently riven by anger and hatred and fear and revenge.

Do I really want to add to that, even at the gain of my own broken self?

Visiting Mrs. D.

A few years ago I was chosen by a local magazine as one of Boston's most eligible singles, whatever the hell that means. After the photo shoot came the interview, and at the end, an apologetic question from the young reporter: "I know one is not supposed to ask a lady this, but we need your age."

My first thought was *No way!* No way in heck was I gonna let this rag print my age for all of Boston to see. Ten seconds later my heart flooded with disappointment, not at the reporter but at myself. I had never been one of those women who believes her face is her treasure, who measures her worth by her looks. Consequently I never worshipped youthfulness or bothered to lie about my age, not even when I first re-entered the dating scene at midlife. If most of my male peers preferred younger companions, oh well: it had nothing to do with me. (What it has to do with, I believe, is not so much sex or fertility as a desire for easy adoration, but never mind.) Younger men apparently found me attractive enough for two to play that game, but the one time I tried having a drink with a twenty-six-year-old man I was bored senseless. I jokingly told him I owned T-shirts older than he was. I didn't mention the T-shirts were more interesting.

Anyway I gave the interviewer my real age and smiled

when he seemed surprised. A few days later I saw the French movie *Amour*. It was brutal and merciless and astonishing, a movie to make most Hollywood spectacles look like the noisy, overwrought child's play they are. *Amour* stared unflinchingly at the reality of aging, at the fact that all of us—all of us, if we're lucky—will slow and wither and diminish, will degrade and finally die, and if we're lucky this will happen with some measure of control and dignity and if we're not it will be really terrible. *Amour* is the kind of movie that would never be made in America, where the denial of death has reached impressive heights. We worship not only youth but adolescence, fifty-year-old women dressing like teenagers, fifty-year-old men on dating sites looking for "a nice girl cause I want to have a family someday." We worship youth and deny aging and shove the reality of death far from sight.

Sometimes I'm frightened by how little connection I have had to death. Grateful too, of course, incredibly grateful, but this cannot go on and maybe all that cushioning will only mean a breaking instead of a bend when the storm inevitably arrives.

Last year I began walking through cemeteries sometimes, trying to face it. They are beautiful, most of them. These people lived, like me, I think. They lived and then they died. That's the way it works. No one gets out any other way.

•

Yesterday I went to visit Mrs. D. Mrs. D is ninety-one years old and dying, though, according to her, not fast enough.

"Every morning I wake up and say, 'Huh. Still here?'" She

tilted her gray eyes to the ceiling. "What's the matter?" she asked God. "Out of room?"

I laughed and Mrs. D joined in. This is one of the things I like most about Mrs. D: she laughs. A lot. The first time I met her we sat and laughed at the Kardashians for an hour. She loves watching the Kardashians, mostly because she can remember who they are and because they are so ridiculous. "Some people like them, some people don't," she said, shrugging. "You don't like them, don't watch. It doesn't matter."

She says that a lot: "It doesn't matter." When I'm with her I realize how much it's true: so much of the nonsense about which we obsess doesn't matter. So much of the nonsense about which I obsess.

I met Mrs. D because I decided one day to volunteer at a hospice. It was a selfish decision; my goal was mostly to make myself confront the reality of death. To pretend you will never die is not only a waste of time and energy but a terrible waste of the gift of being alive. I try my best not to waste.

So I began visiting Mrs. D, who was living out her days in a nondescript skilled nursing facility in a nondescript suburb ten miles from Boston's North End, the Italian neighborhood where she lived the whole of her life. The first time I showed up in her sunny, two-person room she insisted I must be there for someone else.

"Yes, I'm here to see you. I'm a volunteer. Your daughter asked for visitors."

"Not me," she said. "Not me."

Her daughter E visits every day at noon, bringing coffee from Dunkin Donuts or a cannoli as a special treat. They talk and play cards, and E makes sure the chicken or fish or whatever is brought for her mother's lunch is properly cut. Mrs. D has trouble holding a knife but she is well able to feed herself. E is in her seventies but still works part-time and so cannot care for her mother at home. Mrs. D understands. "I want her to have her life. I had my time."

Sometimes when I visit Mrs. D she is depressed. Her room, which she shares with a roommate who is either asleep or absent when I visit, is bright and warm and comfortable but it is just a room. Some of the other clients in the home spend their days socializing in the common room or wandering the hallways (the front door is alarmed to keep dementia patients from wandering outside) but Mrs. D has no interest in making friends or playing board games or otherwise mimicking a life.

"I want to be home," she says.

"I know," I say. We have been trained to listen, to reflect, to console. "What would you want to be doing if you were home?"

"I'd do what *I* want!" This is as close to a flash of temper as I have ever seen from Mrs. D. "Here I have to do what they want, when they want me to do it."

Another day I am surprised to find her in bed instead of the wheelchair where she normally sits. Her feet are hurting. They stretch out strangely at the end of her bed, encased in a pair of the fuzzy socks she is dressed in by the staff every morning. Today's socks are blue and match and her blouse. "I got two good legs and there's nothing wrong with them except they don't work," she says, disgusted. "I can't even go to the bathroom on my own."

Another day she is in bed because her shoulder has been

hurting. "I went to therapy," she says. "Twice. She told me I'd been abusing my side by leaning to the left when I sit in the chair. I know what that means. That means no more therapy. She didn't say that but that's what it means." She shrugs, looks away.

Later she says, "Death is hard. Dying is harder."

Other days, though, she is remarkably cheerful, more cheerful, I think, than anyone has a right to expect, more cheerful than I know I would be. (And often more cheerful than I am when I arrive at the skilled nursing facility, still healthy and stable and relatively young and obsessing over some petty nonsense out in the world). She has a wicked sense of humor. She asks about my hair (I have locs) and I compliment hers, a fluffy brown cloud around her head. "I'm the only one in here with brown hair," she says, and mimics shaking a bottle of dye. "I'm going brown to my grave." She advises me to start dying the tiny gray roots beginning to appear around my face, saying bluntly that they make me look old. When you are dying (and we are all dying) there's no time for BS.

Some of who I am and what I do sticks with her from visit to visit and some does not: she asks over and over again if I have children and what I do for a job. One time I show her the copy of *Invisible Man* I am carrying, having just that morning taught it to a bunch of undergraduates. She says, "So you get paid to sit around and read? That's a pretty good job." No argument there.

The one thing about me that sticks with her is that I am divorced. It came up the first time we met and she brings it up often after that. One time she says, "I remember something about you and a divorce."

"I'm divorced, yes." I smile to show that I am fine.

"I don't like divorce."

"I don't think anybody does, really."

"It happens, though."

"Yes."

"It might happen to me."

I laugh, thinking she is making a joke. But she does not smile. I stop laughing.

"It might happen to you?" We are trained to listen.

"My husband told me he's in love with the nurse. He wants to be with her."

I am pretty sure I read, in her chart, that her husband has been dead for a decade, pretty sure but not positive. "How do you feel about that?"

She shrugs. "Who am I to stand in the way of love?" She says her husband is bringing the papers for her to sign. She asks if there are a lot of papers to sign for a divorce. I tell her, no, not many. It's not so bad.

The week before Christmas we talk about her grandchildren and great-grandchildren, eleven and twelve respectively. "Too many to buy presents for," she says. She asks if my ex-husband come for Christmas dinner. When I say no because he has remarried she says, "Oh. Here I was siding with him and you're the lonely one." This pierces me.

As I am leaving each week Mrs. D asks if I will come again. I tell her I will. But at home I receive a call from the hospice program. "Mrs. D is being removed from the program," the coordinator tells me. "She has exceeded the time limit."

"What does that mean?"

"It's an insurance issue."

"You mean she hasn't died soon enough?"

"It's an insurance issue," she says. "Please do not go see her anymore."

I tell the coordinator I cannot just stop. She tells me that if I go without their approval it will jeopardize their insurance or their license or some such nonsense. We go back and forth for awhile but already I have decided to resign. I will keep visiting Mrs. D on my own auspices. I go once more and we have a lovely visit, watching the Kardashians.

Then I get busy out in the world with petty nonsense and miss three straight weeks and when I return, Mrs. D is gone.

Mothering While Black

Last fall my son turned eighteen. He registered for the draft, finished high school, toured and chose a college on his own. A few months later his sister turned twenty-one, crossing the last of society's finish lines: at sixteen she could drop out of school and have sex, at eighteen, pick up a gun and go to war and now, finally, she can sit in a restaurant and order a glass of wine. My job as a parent is over, essentially. For all intents and purposes, I am done.

Some people don't think so, of course. Some people believe that once a parent always a parent: the job downshifts but never ends. I've seen parents not only dominate their child's college search but also the one for graduate school. I know parents who know more about their child's dating habits than seems appropriate. I know a woman who still does her son's laundry. The son is twenty-nine.

This will not be, I think, the way I operate. I will always be my children's mother, but my days of mothering will soon come to an end. When I mentioned this at a fundraising dinner, the woman next to me offered sympathy for the coming empty nest. When I told her that my son has been in boarding school and so the nest has been empty for a while, she asked how in the world I'd handled it. Her sons were adolescents and already she mourned their growing independence, feared the looming void.

"How have I handled? Let's see: dinner parties. Traveling weekends. Not rushing home after work." I sipped my drink. "It's been a struggle but I am holding up."

She smiled but it was a sad smile. "I'm just worried I'll miss being a mom."

To say I do not miss being *a mom* does not mean I do not love my children. That should go without saying but I know that it does not. (After my third novel, which is about the complexities of motherhood, was published, a white woman showed up to a reading to demand, on the verge of tears, how I could write such things and still call myself a mother. *What about your children?* she cried. *My children are fine,* I said. *What about yours?*) To say I do not miss being *a mom* means mostly that I was never such a creature, which is really just a way of saying I was a certain kind of mother, while the woman at the fundraiser was a different kind. Only one is celebrated and glorified. Only one gets to consider itself the loving ideal.

What makes one person a "mom" and another person "a mother" and a third someone just raising kids? Personality (or perhaps "being" is a better word) is certainly a factor. Writers are both born and made and so are mothers and for me these two states of being did not always easily coincide.

But personality or being is only one factor shaping what kind of mother a woman becomes. The mom at the fundraiser was white and raising white children. She was well-educated, middle-class from birth and now solidly affluent: I got all that over the cheese and wine. Each one of these social forces shaped her mothering as much as love of babies or an affinity with math (she was a CPA). Likewise, being Black and raising Black children, well-educated and poor from birth although no longer, all shaped the mother I became. Being a writer also shaped my mothering. Who we are and what we are is how we are.

Someone once told me that being a mother is like walking: you can try to change it up, but sooner or later you'll fall back into your natural stride. True enough. But the way you stride at any given moment depends as much on the shoes you're wearing and the ground you're covering as anything.

•

When I was a child I had three major ambitions for my life: to be a writer, to not be poor, and to be loved. By the age of twelve or thirteen I understood that babies would complicate, if not outright prevent, each one of those things. That we were poor was obvious, as was the fact that without the five of us children, my mother would not have been. Likewise I could see, from the care and feeding of my younger brother and sister and the babysitting of cousins, that children sucked up your attention and your time, both of which are needed to write. And although it is true that some people have children because they want to be loved,[1] looking for love in that particular place struck me as unwise and undesirable. Children are notoriously unreliable as a source of love. That's not their job.

I had little interest in dolls as a child, though we did have dolls around. The one I remember best had a hole in her mouth into which we stuck a small plastic bottle filled with water and then waited for the water to come out the other end, which happened immediately. That was fun for about ten minutes. Longer-lasting entertainment came from toys that did something: Light Bright, walkie-talkies, SpiroGraph, Shrinky-Dinks.[2] Also from books: I read voraciously, wrote my first story when I was five or six and by middle school knew what I wanted to do.

For my mother, having children was a fact, not a vocation; a duty, not a source of personal enrichment and not particularly fun. The goal was not to *have children*, not anymore than the goal of harvesting seeds is to have seeds or the goal of buying fabric is to have bolts of material lying around; the goal was to raise competent adults. My mother expected no public recognition nor approval for her efforts. She did what she did because that's what you did as a responsible adult, whether you enjoyed it or not.

My mother's philosophy of childrearing prioritized survival, because survival was not guaranteed. Survival is never guaranteed, of course, but pretending is easier for some people than for others; some people live their entire lives believing every breath and every climb on someone's back is their entitlement. We were documented citizens (plus) but also poor and Black (minus, minus) and largely fatherless (minus) and so no such pretense existed for us.

My mother viewed her job as provision of the basics: food, shelter and safety, a religious foundation, education for advancement and education for life. How to clean clothes or cut a chicken, how to rise early and always for a job. How to go to church and sit respectfully. How to shop and cook and advocate for yourself. How not to let the world eat you alive.

There was not a lot of intergenerational playing; adults did not play, not with children anyway. There was not a lot of reading or tending or hugging, not a lot of attention to non-physical wounds. There was not, it must be said, a lot of emotional caretaking; your feelings, whatever they were, did not factor in to whether or not to go to school or rise early for the family paper route or face the embarrassment of food stamps and free lunch. Your feelings would not pay the mortgage or fix the broken furnace or get you first an education and then a job and an escape to a better life. Your feelings, therefore, were largely irrelevant.

I got my period at twelve or thirteen; that I don't even remember precisely might say something about how eager I was to pretend that what was happening was not happening. What was happening, my mother made clear, was my initiation into the lifelong terrors and burden that was being a woman. Chief among these terrors was pregnancy, a mysterious happening that could effectively end your life. This was confirmed when a female relative got pregnant and *dropped out of school.* To me, few things could be more horrible. I loved school: school was safety (then) and ritual and achievement and praise. School was where I thrived. If I needed any reason to avoid pregnancy, there it was.

For the next fifteen years my primary health concern was to not to get pregnant. Even after getting married I was uncertain. My husband and I had agreed we both wanted kids at some vague, unspecific time in the future but I pushed past twenty-eight and twenty-nine and then thirty without that future seeming to arrive. Mostly I'd been trying to escape the poisonous newsroom of the *New York Times* and also write my first novel. Those goals accomplished, I decided to toss my birth control pills and take the risk.

Writers are born, authors are made. My life as an author and as a parent began at the same time.

•

You've all seen this: you're in a restaurant or wandering a museum or waiting to board a plane. A young couple arrives, bearing their progeny before them like the Hope Diamond. The children run rampant, the snacks (and crumbs) are flung around. Mother and Father deliver loving instruction and encouragement at the top of their lungs. All eyes are drawn to them, either in kindness or annoyance, which is precisely the point. Look at us! We're parenting!

Helicopter, free-range or tiger mom: whatever the musical, the spotlight is not on the children. They're just the props, the rest of us the audience. Not all performative parenting is done by mothers, but let's be honest: most of it is. The fathers charging the sidelines at soccer games may be living out some fantasy but it is generally not one of familial perfection. They're trying to prove something to someone but it's not about fatherhood.

At first I thought my lack of interest in this kind of competitive mothering said something about my maternal instinct. There were things I did because they were good for my children that I ended up enjoying (like breastfeeding) and things I did because they were good for my children from which I got no pleasure (like watching endless soccer games) and things I finally ceased doing (watching soccer practice) even when other mothers raised a fishy eye. I took my children to the beach and to the mountains and to every museum in Boston, read to them and talked to them and listened to their child-ish babblings, ironed leaves between wax paper and pasted gin-gerbread homes, oversaw homework and packed lunches and prepared nutritious dinners every night, kept pediatrician vis-its and attended teacher conferences, volunteered in their class-rooms and cut up oranges for their soccer games (Are suburban children really so underfed they cannot survive two hours with-out a snack?) and some of it was fine and a great deal of it was unceasingly tedious and almost none of it fed me intellectually or psychologically or spiritually beyond the satisfaction of a job well done. I got the same feeling raking leaves.

•

There's a story I've told before but here it bears repeating. My daughter was just a few days old when I took her for her first well-baby visit. The pediatrician, a white woman, expressed sur-prise at my daughter's fair complexion, a surprise that did not abate even when I explained that my husband was white. She held her pale forearm to my child's bare stomach and said, "This could almost be my child!" Then, "I'm thinking albino."

The first time I wrote about this incident I used it to illus-trate how frequently white people miscalculated the relationship between myself and my daughter based strictly on the respective tones of our skin. I think I was trying to say something about how quickly race intruded upon my daughter's life.

Twenty years later what I see in that incident is not the pediatrician but myself as a mother, already formed. Since I knew damn well my child was not albino (she had Black hair and hazel eyes) I immediately classified the pediatrician not as an authority but as either incompetent or a threat. I feared she suspected me of kidnapping, had slipped out of the room not to consult her partner, as she said, but to call the cops. When the partner dismissed the albino theory I took my daughter and found another pediatrician. Then I wrote an essay about it and sold it to *The New York Times*.

Which is to say: first I got protective, then angry, then I took action and then I made a story out of it and thus controlled the narrative. And when my daughter was old enough I told her that story so that she would know. Who we are and what we are shape the mothers that we become.

Here's another story.

When my children were young I met a Black woman in our little suburban town whose children, years older than mine, had all attended private schools. This struck me as strange: why else did people live in the suburbs except for the schools? Why would educated Black parents not want to support public education?

"You'll see," the woman said. "And, by the way, I'm not the only one."

I believed in public education and so in we jumped. We chose the town's one integrated elementary school (the other three were 96, 92 and 90 percent white), met the teachers, supported the dynamic Black principal, joined the PTO. We tackled racial imbalances in the school's French immersion program, launched innovative programs to increase parental involvement in the school, tackled racial imbalances in standardized test scores and in the advanced learning tracks. For seven or eight years I went to every PTO meeting, every back-to-school night, every school board meeting. I worked on ballot measures and referendums, got involved in the hiring of a new superintendent, one who was energetic and conscientious and who saw the district's obvious racial inequities and set out to change them. Naturally, the shit hit the fan.[3]

To say the racism I heard from my fellow townsmen and women at meetings was thinly-veiled would be generous. At one meeting, a white woman stood at the microphone and cried at the thought of her precious progeny attending school "with those children." Another suggested our school—which we all loved, by the way—was overrun with "discipline problems." As if the hallways were rife with roaming gangs of armed first-graders.

But they won, of course: the integration plan was shelved, as was another plan to reduce clear racial disparities in the advanced classes at the middle school. The justice-seeking superintendent was run out of town, replaced with a go-along, get-along official. Finally I saw what the Black mother from years before had warned me about. Those Black parents weren't just protecting their children, they were also preserving their own energy. Parenting while Black is an exhausting job.

Imagine (if you are not a Black parent) eighteen years

of running interference, plowing through an endless field of
people and institutions trying to tackle your precious child.
It doesn't matter that some of the attempted hits are minor
(stupid comments about hair or background or skin tone) or
distant (relentless racist attacks against the first Black president) or unintentional (biased discipline).[4] It doesn't matter if
your opponents are smiling in your face at the school commit-
tee meeting or failing to treat your child's asthma[5] or screaming "Nigger!" from their car. It doesn't matter if you live north
or south or east or west or if the child is female or male. Tamir
Rice. Michael Brown. Renisha McBride. The list goes on.

Imagine (if you are not a Black parent) holding your breath
every time your child stepped out of your protective embrace
into a world not just randomly dangerous but specifically hostile. Imagine (if you are not a Black parent) always having to
think through the possible consequences of simple actions, like
sending your teen son out to the driveway after dark to retrieve
something from the car and then running out behind him in a
panic because you fear the police in your suburban little town
will see a Black man entering a car at night and weaponize. Last
year, while visiting friends on the Cape, I called home to check
on my then seventeen-year-old son, who was not answering the
phone. After awhile I began to worry. My friend, who is white
and a mother of adult children, suggested I call the local police
and ask them to check on my son. Her blissful unawareness of
what a terrifying suggestion that was to a Black mother sad-
dened but did not surprise me. I called another friend.

Who you are and what you are shapes your parenting;
the ground you're covering determines your gait. When my

daughter was born I knew very little about mothering, but quite a lot about surviving as a Black woman in America. I knew my children would have to be grounded, clear-eyed and resilient. I knew they needed as broad a perspective as possible. I knew they needed to be able to fight for themselves and stand on their own.

I filled our house with Black history and Black heroes, hung posters of Frederick Douglass and Harriet Tubman and Malcolm X. I bought Black books and Black toys and Black dolls (what dolls I bought). I joined a Black church not simply for the religious instruction but to immerse my children in Black history and culture (my children know how to clap on the down beat and speak properly to their elders and sing the words to "Lift Every Voice and Sing") and to surround them with loving, positive Black role models. When we encountered the snake of racism or simple racial ignorance (the white guy at our local park who questioned my right to be there, the white receptionist at the vet who asked if my children were "mulatto") I grabbed it by the neck and laid it on the table and made my children look at it. Sometimes they wanted to discuss what had happened; many times, they did not. They also didn't want to wear their seatbelts or clean their rooms or get vaccinated at the pediatrician every year: what has that got to do with anything?

In seventh grade my son said, of our very good public middle school, "This school is holding me back." The next year he asked to apply to boarding schools. I didn't want him to go; he was my baby and also I had attended boarding schools. I knew how tough they could be. But I also knew they could challenge him and he wanted that challenge. I said yes. Not one Black parent I know questioned this decision but several white parents did. "Oh, I could never send my child away from home!" said one woman I met at a party. She raised an eyebrow. "You read so much about the things that happen at boarding schools."

I laughed at her. "You think *things* don't happen at your local high school? Pretty sure life happens everywhere. I've tried to prepare my son for avoiding trouble, or handling it."

In tenth grade my son said he wanted to spend his junior year living in France.[6] Again, some white parents I know were aghast: *Oh my God, aren't you scared to let him go? France is so dangerous!"*

This time I didn't laugh, because that level of insular privilege is no laughing matter for the rest of us. Gun violence, resurgent racist violence, over-policing of young Black men. In the United States, young Black men are between nine and sixteen times more likely than other people to be killed by police.[7] But France is dangerous?

The illusion of safety is something no Black parent can afford. I let my child go to France, where he gained fluency in French, travelled throughout Europe and became a citizen of the world. My daughter later spent a semester in Denmark and did the same and I supported her because this much I know: the bigger your world, the smaller the chance you'll believe the lies they tell you. The bigger your world, the more impossible it is for anyone to take it away from you.

Not that they won't still try. Here's a third and final story. My son was graduated from Phillips Exeter Academy in June. I think his lowest grade over four years was a B+. Made the dean's list every trimester he was there. Spent his junior year living in

France. Participated in Model U.N. in Geneva. Was kind to his host family siblings, who adored him. Rowed varsity crew. Missed one question on his SATs. Was accepted at every Ivy League school to which he applied. Among other things.

My son just texted me that people have been telling him the only reason he is now at Harvard is because he is Black. This is neither novel nor unexpected--every school since junior high I have ever attended, every institution at which I have ever worked, every accomplishment I have ever earned someone has attempted to taint withe same, tired accusation -- and yet it broke my heart. I cried, reading my son's text. I am crying now. Because he also said, "And I know I shouldn't believe it but sometimes I do a little bit."

Is it possible to raise a whole Black child in America? Is it fucking possible? I did my best for my children, tried hard and daily first to protect them from, and them to arm them against, the constant physical, emotional and psychological assaults of white supremacy. My precious daughter and my precious son know who they are and from whence they came, as Uncle Jimmy said. They know Douglass and Jacobs and DuBois, Hurston and Malcolm and Stokely. They certainly know Uncle Jimmy. There is more for them to know but they know much. They have been raised in so-called progressive Massachusetts, both lived briefly outside the United States. They know about white suprem-acy, because I have never ceased talking about it, although, of course, they don't really know because you never really know until you have been battling it awhile and until this moment I have been taking most of their battles but now that will change. They know my story and the story of my siblings and the story of my mother and they know how much we have all had to do and be to get to where we are and they know I KNOW I have a right to be here. They know all of this. And yet.

Was pulling my children from the local public school system the right thing to do? Unlike some of the Black parents I left behind, I possessed the educational and economic capital (i.e time) to fight the system and perhaps improve it for all children. But doing battle is exhausting; I focused instead on stabilizing after divorce, fighting depression and navigating the shark-infested waters of academia. It felt like all I could do. It had to be enough.

Who I am and what I am made me the mother that I was and none of it makes me a better or worse mother than that woman at the fundraiser. The perfect mother is a myth, which, like all myths, reflects and amplifies and shapes the culture in which it was born. In this case, the case of the American Mom, proximity to the myth is more accessible to certain kinds of people, based as much upon their economic and social positions as on their maternal instincts. Which is one of the reasons we should do away with it.

Loving your own children makes you neither righteous nor virtuous. Looking out for your own, fulfilling your responsibility to human beings you chose or brought to life, caring for the people within your tribe: none of this makes you a saint. Contrary to bumper stickers and mommy blogs, motherhood is not inherently noble and neither are mothers.[8]

If we were, the world would be a much better place.

Womanish

I. Age does not a woman make.

A friend from high school asks, "What does the phrase *middle-aged crisis* mean to you?" He is white, gay, handsome and worldly, a lovely man in his fifties now entering a period of questioning and ennui.

"Nothing," I tell him. "It means nothing to me, as I had all my crises in my twenties and thirties. I'm pretty much through."

This is, I know, not helpful to my friend but is accurate: I am content to be the age I am. When my colleagues in the university declare how much they enjoy being around young people because it keeps them young I am befuddled; it's like saying one enjoys sleeping because it keeps you dreaming. I enjoy sleeping because eventually I wake up. Youth isn't so much wasted on the young as cursed upon them. Wise people outgrow the curse, but, of course, most people in America (or anywhere) are not wise. In America most people outlive the biological fact of being young without ever outgrowing the dumb, dangerous state of innocence. Innocence is a state to which a mature and thoughtful human should neither aspire nor cling. What's really wasted in America is adulthood. We don't have nearly enough adults. Especially men. But that's another essay.

I loved the movie *Girls Trip* as much as anyone and I

167

get the concept of in-groups reclaiming words but kindly do not call me a girl (or nigger or cunt, for that matter). Being a woman is an achievement, like earning a doctorate, only harder: I have no interest in downplaying the accomplishment or in clinging to some imagined state of innocence. Once a waitress (white and younger, if not precisely young), greeted myself and a sister friend by asking, "How you girls doing today?" Politely I responded, "We're doing well, thanks, but we are not girls. Could you bring some water, please?" Granted, when my sister friend asked, after the embarrassed waitress left, "Girl, what are you doing?" I did not object.

Do I contradict myself? Very well, I contradict myself. Womanish.

•

II. When I was a child . . .

When I was a child I knew precisely how children were treated because I saw it on TV. They were spoken to gently, listened to respectfully, learned from humbly, laughed along with and hugged. Since very little of that happened to the small people in my neighborhood I didn't think of us as children. We were more like humans-in-training: fed, clothed and sheltered, instructed when necessary and ignored as much as possible. This was not cruel or unloving it was simply a different way of parenting, a way that stemmed not from the goal of *having* children but from the goal of *raising* adults. We weren't treated like the children on television because we were essentially in training for womanhood and manhood right from the start.

Likewise, although I understood myself as female, I rarely thought of myself as a girl. Girlishness was something that belonged to white people, to Buffy and Cissy and Jan and Marsha Brady, to Ann Margaret and Mary Tyler Moore, a hair-tossing, wide-eyed, carefree way of being in the world. Life for me and my mother and my sisters and my aunts was just life, but life for girls was like a cakewalk in the park: music played, you paraded around in a pretty dress and had people hand you sweet things. It was certainly possible for Black girls to be girl-ish in this fashion, but I only knew one: a friend named Catania.

Nor were there many cultural models to observe. The few Black girls on television (our central constructor of reality) pro-jected maturity and sassiness not sweetness and innocence: Tootie on *The Facts of Life*, Thelma on *Good Times*, Shirley and Dee on *That's My Mama*. In 2017 the Center on Poverty and Inequality at Georgetown Law published a study showing that adults of all races view Black girls as more mature, less innocent and less in need of protection than white girls the same age. This "adultification" begins as young as five.[1]

So I understood myself not as a girl but definitely as female. To be female meant life would be both hard and haz-ardous; my job was to avoid the hazards I could and endure the ones I could not. The good news was that God had given women the strength to do precisely that. My mother backed away from nothing because she was a woman: not car repairs or house repairs or child repairs, not sorting mail at the post office, nor tossing stacks of newspapers into our ink-stained car to deliver before dawn. When I was twelve she piled the five of us children into the car and drove from Memphis to

Sacramento in search of opportunity. Six months later, finding obstacles, she drove us back. She fought vermin, maintained the law, threatened bad boyfriends (her daughters, not her own— she never dated) and whatever help she received along the way came mostly from women: her sisters and mother and aunts. My uncles were good-hearted but mostly defeated men who came through with only the occasional roof patch or lent male presence. Mostly the women were on their own.

I never expected anyone to help me because I was a girl and they rarely did, so things worked out. Being tall (five-ten by high school) and Black and quiet made people think I was far more capable and confident than I really was, which, of course, meant I had to become those things. When my first boyfriend joked about not being able to carry me if something happened it broke my heart, but I didn't tell him that. We met at the elite white boarding school to which I had earned a scholarship and to which I had to travel myself. I learned how to navigate both planes and buses and to never pack more than I could bear.

Being female also meant having a female body, a ticking time bomb of odors and blood and the sexual attention of men and, inevitably and worst of all, pregnancy. Sex was dirty and dangerous and something no decent woman should yearn for; having a baby meant the meaningful end of whatever dreams you might hold for yourself. Unless, of course, your dream was only to have babies; such women existed, we knew, but they were not respected in my house. Being a mother was something you did when you couldn't put it off any longer, like menstruate. It was not something to look forward to or aspire towards or define yourself by. It was something you really wanted to be.

This is what it meant to be woman in the world of my youth: serious and responsible and in charge. You took care of business, which meant taking care of you and yours. You weren't going to get a lot of help and you would most certainly face some obstacles, both because you were a woman and because you were Black. That was just life and there was no getting around it. The only way through was through.

The women of my childhood were serious and responsible and capable and in charge but not audacious. They liked food and music and the Holy Spirit but not dance or roundness or the moon. They did not, for the most part, love themselves. No one had ever told them they should. The women of my childhood were undoubtedly women but they were not necessarily womanish. Their definition was narrower, emphasizing hardship and responsibility and obligation, but not fullness or roundness or love. It often involved relief and gratitude and sometime happiness but not often joy. It involved astonishing resilience but not much audacity.

When I was a child I spoke like a child and understood like a child and thought as that child but when I became a woman I sensed that was not enough.

•

III. Venus and Mars

To be womanish is to be a womanist and vice versa. That goes without saying.

To be womanish is also to have zero time for accusations of being anti-man. As it happens, some of my best friends have penises, or so I assume. I love them, respect them, admire their humanity. So that takes care of that.

To be womanish is to be astonished when encountering misogyny, if not precisely surprised. It's like coming across a man polluting the ocean because he's afraid to swim. Any Black girl growing up in the traditional Black church understands sexism, at least on some level, but my twenties and thirties were largely focused on dodging the bullets of white racism. For whatever reason—physical appearance, obliviousness, luck—I largely eluded sexual harassment in the workplace and social sphere (as opposed to street harassment, which no woman eludes). Bosses never hit on me, touched me, made inappropriate remarks. One or two colleagues did but these attempts were more fumbling than aggressive; one of them I only recognized in retrospect. I knew my career as a journalist might have gone further and faster had I been a man but the major frustrations, entrapments, obstacles I dealt with in newsrooms seemed unattached to my being a woman. They seemed attached mostly to people being assholes, and also to me being Black.

Thus I entered mid-life dating wildly underestimating everyday misogyny. If you want to encounter seething anger at, and barely-concealed hatred of, women (besides, you know, politics and the general world) check out Plenty of Fish and OKCupid and also Match. At first it seemed so incongruous— men seeking women while simultaneously bashing them— I couldn't quite make it out. Okay, your marriage ended: perhaps you contributed to the breakdown? Okay, your ex-wife cheated: does that make all women filthy whores? Okay, you grew up without sisters and do not have a daughter: does that really render you incapable of understanding that I am not simply a walking vagina, that my body contains a heart and mind just like yours? (Well . . .) Perhaps the reason it took so long for me to grasp that some men do not think of women as fully human is that for all the disgusted, dismayed or dismissing-of-men women that I have known, not one has held men to be inhuman. Not one.

Women may dislike men or even hate them, but the bulk of women are fully aware of men's humanity. For one thing, we give birth to them. More critically, men present a real and present danger to women, and, as Black people know, to survive a danger, you must *see* it for what it is. Going further, what's the worst thing a woman can do to a man, according to the anti-woman crowd? Deny access to her body by withholding sex and/or using sex to manipulate men. The denying access charge we will not dignify, but that some women sexually or emotionally manipulate men is undeniable. But here's the thing: to manipulate a being, as opposed to control that being, requires attentiveness to the being's emotional and psychological needs, which in turn requires, however grudging, an acknowledgement that said being *has* emotional and psychological needs. You control a car or a cow. You train a dog. The only thing you manipulate is a human being.

The misogyny revealed on online dating sites is naked in its source, which is not a sense of superiority but clearly one of terror: what people hate is what they fear. Nobody hates a rock until it turns to lava, or the wind until a hurricane. Black people have always known this. What white America fears is *not* Black people but the loss of white identity, privilege and position the Black presence demands and also the spiritual and cultural power Black survival has produced. What men fear is the power of women: intellectual, psychological, spiritual and, yes, sexual. In some ways, this is understandable: the power of a fully-realized woman is palpable and daunting.

Or, if one is not afraid, quite wonderful.

•

IV. A letter to my daughter on the 156th anniversary of the birth of Ida B. Wells.

Dear Daughter,

I have begun this letter twenty times and deleted it twenty times and I'm probably not done. I keep seeing your beautiful face, which is more the face of your father than my own, thus proving what the old folks say: women make the boys, men make the girls. But I know that inside of you there's a lot of me, for worse and for better. Mostly you are your own best thing.

This is the part of the letter where I am supposed to explain how I got from A to Z or maybe (because I hope I'm not quite yet at the end) from A to N or O or P. Here is where I locate some crisis that taught me a lesson, some turning point or moment of epiphany to which I can attribute the woman I now am. Except I can't seem to find this mystical turning point. "It's easy to see the beginnings of things but harder to see the endings" wrote Joan Didion, and, I might add, really tricky to make out the path between. It's like trying to give directions to a place you found only by leaving other places behind and wandering. Or running, as the case may be.

From your vantage point the adults around you probably seem like Athena, sprung full-grown from some mysterious point in time. But the only thing I knew when I left home for boarding school at sixteen, besides the fact that I was ambivalent about leaving home for boarding school (it was largely my mother's idea), was that I no longer wanted to be poor. I wasn't aiming for womanishness because I didn't know womanishness existed at which to be aimed. I didn't aspire to fullness or complexity, did not aim for audacity and love and life. All I knew was that poverty sucked and I would prefer not to continue indulging it. Which is not to say I wanted riches: I had no interest in mansions or expensive car or designer clothes (and still do not). What I wanted was simply freedom from the stress, instability and exhausting mental, physical and spiritual costs of poverty. How can I explain it to you, since you've never been poor? Here's a story: last week, after a long day at the office, I waited at the bus stop with a crowd of people as the rain poured down and the bus did not come. Time passed. The crowd expanded. Tempers rose. You know I commute by bus because I support public transportation and worry about climate change and because the parking in downtown Boston is ridiculous. But after twenty-five minutes of waiting, when the crowd had grown far too large for one bus and people grew angry it occurred to me that I could simply walk through the train station and take a cab. The $10 or would not break me; it wouldn't even make a dent. That's what I wanted.

I also wanted to write, was, in fact, already writing. But I didn't think it was possible to do so for a living, and that came first. One of my greatest joys is that you have not grown up with the threat of limited horizons or with the hot breath of poverty on your neck but I have to tell you: these can be great motivators. Do you know Satchel Paige? He said: Don't look back. Something might be gaining on you.

I know you know Ida B. Wells-Barnett. She was amazing: born in Holly Springs, Mississippi, where our own family is from to enslaved parents six months before Emancipation, the oldest of eight children and surely the first in her family to attend school. Dropped out of school at sixteen to support her entire family after her parents both died in the yellow fever epidemic of 1878. Became a school teacher and then later, in Memphis (another connection) an editor and investigative journalist. Fearlessly documented and denounced the epidemic of lynching spreading across the south post-Reconstruction and campaigned relentlessly for equal protection under the law.

It's tempting to read about women like Wells and believe she had some grand plan for moving from slavery to the kind of centeredness and confidence and clarity required to challenge an entire society, that she knew where she was headed the moment she set out. My guess is no. My guess is that during those moments when the ocean was rough she poured her energy into staying afloat. But when the ocean was calm, instead of just drifting or gazing up at the sun she took the opportunity to look deeper. That, I think, is the key.

I can't, my precious daughter, give you a recipe for achieving womanishness. At best I can tell you some of the ingredients I used. For example, for whatever reason, I was pretty good at learning from other people's mistakes, misfortunes and misunderstandings. Most people don't, you know. It's strange.

Growing up we all see, we think, so clearly what's wrong with our parents, our society, the world. We swear to be better, or at least to be different, but usually that vow is forgotten and even when it isn't, the different turns out to be much the same or even worse. Which is perhaps the primary reason humanity has not progressed further: the world is full of both guidance and warnings, in both life and literature, and yet most people insist on stumbling blindly along, figuring it out for themselves. Sure, life is a serious teacher but she's not the fastest, most efficient one in school. Or the only one.

The issue, of course, is that to learn from someone else's mistakes one must first refrain from judgment. Judgment clouds understanding; if you don't believe that, just surf Twitter some afternoon. To learn from someone else's mistake one must first observe that person's humanity. Then see how their misstep has damaged it. Teaching literature to undergraduates is incredibly fulfilling because of the consciousness-expanding possibility literature creates, but my biggest challenge is often to restrain students from leaping to judgments about literary characters after the most superficial of readings. They label a character as X-ist, declare, "I don't like him" and close the book. *What the hell has like got to do with anything?* I ask and make them open it again.

But I know you get that, my daughter: you are so much smarter, more perceptive and more thoughtful than I was at your age. Still young and yet already a woman.

Your womanishness is going to be an amazing thing.

Love,

Mom

Better than the Alternative

The weekend before my fiftieth birthday I badly burned my hand. It was stupid and embarrassing; walking around two days later bandaged like a mummy I tried to think of a sellable lie. Cooking seemed the most likely explanation. Boiling water. Stirring grits.

What really happened was I decided, for some bizarre reason, to try to wax my legs at home. There's this kit, see; you get it at the CVS. A little tub of wax you heat in the microwave for thirty seconds. But my microwave is old and spotty and thirty seconds left the wax as cold and stiff as Mitt Romney. So I popped it back in for another thirty seconds, or maybe forty or forty-five. You can see where this is going.

The microwave dings. Distracted, unfocused, I reach up and pop open the door. Grab the tub. Yank it out.

Because I am me and because I am writer and because this happened a week before the start of my sixth decade on this earth I spent the next few days searching for the meaning to be made from this, for the metaphor to present itself.

Point One: I got the kit on a lark but also to save money; even after a few decades out of poverty I still have trouble spending money on frivolous things, especially for myself. (A woman I know recently showed me her red-heeled Louboutin (or whatever) shoes, crowing with delight about how they'd been on her bucket list. I could spend $1000 on shoes if I really wanted; the day I do is the day the bucket takes a kick.)

Point Two: I was rushing, mind on a hundred things. I'd already gone for a run that morning, worked in the garden, got the kids off to various places, walked the dog. I had the vacuum out for next, nail polish for my toes jammed into the pocket of my shirt, a plan to make the supermarket by six. I was rushing and impatient and hyper-productive, crankily getting things done because if I didn't who the hell would?

Point Three: I was preparing for a date, seeking to impress, determined to earn love, as if love needed earning, not yet bothering to determine if the object of my quest was worthwhile. Which he wasn't.

Point Four: I was alone. No one to rely on except myself.

When the wax first hit I felt a flush of heat, a biting sting. I dropped the tub, splattering everywhere (and probably cursing; I don't recall). Get to the sink, I told myself, and did, running cold water over my arm for maybe a second. Change your clothes, grab your keys, get to the hospital.

No idea why I thought I needed to change my pants; they were the same, grungy, less-than-presentable tights I'd run in, but, really, who cares? (Later I'd notice the fist-sized hole the wax had burned in one thigh and think: better them than me).

Even with the changing, though, from the time I grabbed the wax to the time I was in my car, aiming it one-handed down the streets of my little suburban town was maybe three minutes — four minutes, tops. I was calm, I did not panic, was not hysterical. Bits of my skin had curled back from my arm like bark from a birch and, through the wax, I could see dermis, subcutaneous tissue, layers of muscle and fat . . . or so it seemed. By the time I pulled my car responsibly into the hospital parking lot the stinging had stopped and the pain gone mute. Walking inside I thought: either in about ten minutes I'm going to be screaming. Or this is really, really bad.

Anyway, long story short: the ER doc said it might be third-degree and I might need a skin graft. He offered me oxycodone for the pain and I was glad he offered it because I know studies show Black patients are routinely under treated for pain in emergency rooms but I declined because that stuff scares me to bits. They gave me Motrin; I swallowed it. They removed the wax, cleaned the burn, wrapped me up and sent me off. Two days later the folks at the burn clinic told me it wasn't, in fact, a third-degree burn, just a bad second-degree. No skin grafts needed. I would be fine, thank the Lord.

Before all this happened I'd been feeling a little blue about my birthday. I fear death less than aging badly but I fear regret most of all. I've lived a life of extraordinary blessings, have done just about all the things I've wanted to *do*. What I still yearn for are mostly things I want to experience, things—or, rather, experiences—which are outside of my control. Experiences for which I will just have to wait and which may never come.

But there's nothing like a second-degree burn to snap you out of your self-pity and set you straight. It's not so much than it could have been worse (though it can always be worse) as that whatever it is, it is. And that's okay.

One of the gifts of being a writer is that everything is material. In the end I not only told everyone the truth about my burn but I wrote this essay, transmuting my embarrassment into something else, something with meaning. Or so I hope. "Your silence will not protect you," said Audre Lorde. I guess I understand that much.

The day I turned fifty, I went back to the hospital for a checkup. I had dutifully followed the wound care instructions, adding only some vitamin E oil to the daily ritual. Trust me: vitamin E is like some kind of crazy, miracle thing.

The nurse examined my hand, turning it this way and that way, checking her notes to make sure she had the date of the injury correct.

"Looks great," she said. "You're a fast healer."

I don't know about fast. But, yes, I heal.

Notes

ALRIGHT, CUPID

1. During the 1940s, psychologists Kenneth Bancroft Clark and his wife, Mamie Phipps Clark designed a test to study the psychological effects of segregation on black children using black and white dolls. The results of this research were used by the NAACP Legal Defense Fund in arguments before the U.S. Supreme Court in the landmark desegregation case Oliver Brown v. Board of Education of Topeka, Kansas.

2. *A Girl like Me* is a 2005 documentary by Kiri Davis in which the young filmmaker recreates the doll test.

3. Christian Rudder, "Race and Attraction: 2009-2014," OKCupid Blog, 10 Sept. 2014, https://theblog.okcupid.com/race-and-attraction-2009-2014-107dcbb4f060.

4. Which is in no way a criticism or critique of the lovely and talented actresses who play these roles: I, for one, adore Tracey Ellis Ross.

5. Interestingly, when Black women, in a recent burst of visibility, are cast as the love interest of white men in television shows (and commercials!) the actresses tend to have (for Hollywood) darker, richer skin tones. See, among others, *The Flash* and *Sleepy Hollow*, which should have been a love story but stupidly was not.

6. Kristen Bialik, "Key facts about race and marriage, 50 years after Loving v. Virginia," *Fact Tank*, Pew Research Center, 12 June 2017, http://www.pewresearch.org/fact-tank/2017/06/12/key-facts-about-race-and-marriage-50-years-after-loving-v-virginia/ (accessed 10 Aug 2018).

7. Ashley Crossman, "Definition of the Sociological Imagination and Overview of the Book," ThoughtCo, 23 April 2018, https://www. thoughtco.com/sociological-imagination-3026756.

8. The upside of being invisible/ugly as a girl is being forced to build self-esteem on something other than looks. This makes aging a helluva lot easier.

9. Meg Butler, "Why Online Dating Doesn't Work for Black Women," *MadameNoire*, 13 Jan. 2015, http://madamenoire.com/502861/online-dating-doesnt-work-for-Black-women/ (accessed 10 Aug. 2018).

10. Andrew Ofstehage, Ankita Gandhi, Jared Sholk, Anne Radday, Colette Stanzler, "Empowering Victims of Domestic Violence," Social Impact Research, http://www.rootcause.org/docs/Resources/Research/Empowering-Victims-of-Domestic-Violence/Empowering%20Victims%20of%20Domestic%20Violence-%20Social%20Issue%20Report.pdf.

11. Lawanna Lynn Campbell, "Myths About Domestic Violence and Domestic Abuse," ThoughtCo. https://www.thoughtco.com/domestic-violence-myths-3533789 (accessed August 14, 2018).

BECKY AND ME

1. And sometimes, more precisely, an arrogant white woman.

2. "With very few exceptions, I feel that white people will betray me; that in the final analysis, they'll give me up . . . It's just a kind of a constant vigilance and awareness that maybe these relationships can go just so far." —*Toni Morrison, interview with Ed Bradley, "60 Minutes," 8 March 1998.*

3. Daniel Cox, Juhem Navarro-Rivera, Robert P. Jones, "Race, Religion, and Political Affiliation of Americans' Core Social Networks," Public Religion Research Institute, 3 Aug. 2016, https://www.prri.org/research/poll-race-religion-politics-americans-social-networks/ (accessed 23 May 2018).

4. New Hampshire state trooper, 2014.

5. Exeter, NH, circa 1981, Greensboro, NC circa 1989, Philadelphia, circa 1999.

6. Boston, Greensboro, Philadelphia, New York.

7. Madeline Farber, "3 Reasons Why the Gender Pay Gap Still Exists," *Fortune*, 3 April 2017, http://fortune.com/2017/04/03/equal-pay-day-2017-wage-gap/ (accessed 23 May 2018).

8. Bridget Ansel, "The Vast Wealth Gap Between Black and White women in the United States," Washington Center for Equitable Growth, 31 Jan. 2017, http://equitablegrowth.org/equitablog/the-vast-wealth-gap-between-Black-and-white-women-in-the-united-states (accessed May 28, 2018).

9. United States Census Bureau, *Educational Attainment in the United States: 2015*, Washington, DC: U.S. Department of Commerce, Economics and Statistics Administration, March 2016, www.census.gov/content/dam/Census/library/publications/2016/demo/p20-578.pdf (accessed 12 Aug. 2018).

10. US Bureau of Labor Statistics, *Labor Force Characteristics by Race and Ethnicity, 2014*, Washington, DC: BLS Reports, Nov 2015, www.bls.gov/opub/reports/race-and-ethnicity/archive/labor-force-characteristics-by-race-and-ethnicity-2014.pdf (accessed 12 Aug. 2018).

11. US Department of Education, *The Condition of Education 2017*, Washington, DC: National Center for Education Statistics, May 2018, https://nces.ed.gov/fastfacts/display.asp?id=61 (accessed 12 Aug. 2018).

12. Victoria M. Massie, "White Women Benefit Most from Affirmative Action—and Are Among Its Fiercest Opponents," Vox, 23, June 2016, https://www.vox.com/2016/5/25/11682950/fisher-supreme-court-white-women-affirmative-action (acessed 10 Aug 2018).

13. Jennifer Hochschild, "Affirmative Action as Culture War," *The Cultural Territories of Race: Black and White Boundaries,* ed. Michèle Lamont. University of Chicago Press and Russell Sage Foundation (Chicago, New York: 1999).

14. Kristen Bellstrum, "Sheryl Sandberg: These Are the Biggest

Obstacles for Women Trying to 'Lean In'," *Fortune*, 27 Sept. 2016, http://fortune.com/2016/09/27/sheryl-sandberg-women-in-the-workplace/ (accessed 14 Aug. 2018).

15. Lauren Arnold, "Opinion: White feminism fails 'angry black' first lady, but coddles Melania Trump," CUIndependent, 28 Feb. 2017, https://cuindependent.com/2017/02/28/opinion-white-feminism-fails-defend-angry-Black-first-lady-coddles-melania-trump-michelle-obama/ (accessed 14 Aug. 2018).

16. Brittney Cooper, "Lay off Michelle Obama: Why white feminists need to lean back," *Salon*, 29 Nov. 2013, http://www.salon.com/2013/11/29/lay_off_michelle_obama_why_white_feminists_need_to_lean_back/ (accessed 14 Aug. 2018).

17. Kathryn Kish Sklar, *Women's Rights Emerges within the Antislavery Movement 1830-1870, A Brief History with Documents,* (New York: Bedford/St. Martin's, 2000).

18. Sklar, pg. 73.

19. Sklar, pg. 75.

20. Michael Janofsky, "At Million Woman March, Focus Is on Family," *The New York Times,* 26 Oct. 1997, https://www.nytimes.com/1997/10/26/us/at-million-woman-march-focus-is-on-family.html (accessed 16 Aug. 2018).

21. Why do white women always declare how much they love us? What has that love ever accomplished? Who needs that kind of love?

22. Untrue. White women, though lacking important rights, were not property.

23. Ridiculous. Even in most states in the south unmarried free women (i.e. white women for the most part) had the legal right to live where they pleased, support themselves, enter into contracts, sue and be sued, write wills, buy and sell real estate and accumulate personal property, including slaves. Even after a free woman (i.e white, for the most part) married and lost the right to own personal property independent of her husband (unless they signed a special contract) she maintained important rights to real property, i.e. the land and build-

ings that constituted real wealth. She also maintained the right to dower, i.e. to be supported after her husband died. She also, of course, maintained the right not to be sold to another human being.

24. Even more fascinating are student reactions to *The Confessions of Nat Turner*. White students who have sadly shaken their heads over the raping, whipping and killing of Black men, women, and children outlined by Jacobs, Douglass, Northrup, and Equiano grow enraged at Turner's killing of White women and children. Every semester at least fifty percent denounce Turner's rebellion. One student declared, with all sincerity, "Violence is never the answer. They could have staged a strike or something."

25. Kyle Scott Claus, "City of Boston Employee Wins $10.9 Million in Treasury Department Discrimination Suit," *Boston Magazine,* 23 Oct. 2015, http://www.bostonmagazine.com/news/blog/2015/10/23/city-of-boston-discrimination-suit/ (accessed 14 Aug. 2018).

26. Liz Spayd, "Preaching the Gospel of Diversity, but Not Following It," *New York Times, 17 Dec. 2016,* https://www.nytimes.com/2016/12/17/public-editor/new-york-times-diversity-liz-spayd-public-editor.html?mcubz=1 (accessed 14 Aug. 2018).

ON SELF-DELUSION

1. Joan Didion, *The Year of Magical Thinking* (New York: Knopf, 2005).

2. Gordon Marino, "Stop Kidding Yourself: Kierkegaard on Self-Deception," *Philosophy Now,* Issue 66, 2008, https://philosophynow.org/issues/66/Stop_Kidding_Yourself_Kierkegaard_on_Self-Deception, (accessed 01 May 2018).

3. Joan Didion, "Why I Write," *The New York Times,* 5 Dec 1976, 270.

4. "Happy Independence Day! Hah! To who? Neither I nor my ancestors were liberated on this day. What hypocrisy!" Kim McLarin, excerpt from diary, 4 July 1978.

5. Oliver Smith, "Which Nationalities Work the Longest Hours?" *The Telegraph,* 7 Feb. 2018, https://www.telegraph.co.uk/travel/maps-

and-graphics/nationalities-that-work-the-longest-hours/ (accessed 23 May 2018).

6. Chauncey Devega, "The plague of angry white men: How racism, gun culture & toxic masculinity are poisoning America," *Salon*, https://www.salon.com/2015/07/07/the_plague_of_angry_white_ men_how_racism_gun_culture_toxic_masculinity_are_poisoning_ america_in_tandem/ (accessed 23 May 2018).

7. *Kill Bill* is an exception, a cartoony-violent Tarantino thing onto itself.

MOTHERING WHILE BLACK

1. Many people get dogs for the same reason. Dog love is equally slavish but far more consistent.

2. I did desperately want (and eventually got!) an Easy-Bake oven but that was because by the age of six I already loved to cook, not because I fantasized about being a wife and mother.

3. Joseph Pereira, School Integration Efforts Face Renewed Opposition, *The Wall Street Journal*, 11 Oct. 2007, https://www.wsj.com/ articles/SB119204532864854966 (accessed 10 Aug. 2018).

4. Dick Startz, "Schools, Black Children and Corporal Punishment," The Brown Center Chalkboard, 14 Jan. 2016, https://www.brookings. edu/blog/brown-center-chalkboard/2016/01/14/schools-Black-children-and-corporal-punishment/ (accessed 04 May 2018).

5. Robert Preidt, "Asthma Much More Lethal for Black Children, Study Finds," *HealthDay News*, 4 Mar. 2017, https://www.webmd. com/asthma/news/20170304/asthma-much-more-lethal-for-Black-children-study-finds (accessed 10 Aug. 2018).

6. *"I liked Zurich and I think I want to learn German next. Switzerland is really pretty and really sane, unlike so much of the world. But it's expensive there. I liked Vienna even better. You know how the main library in Boston is so beautiful? In Vienna they have this library that makes the Boston library look like a Quickie-Mart. It's magnificent. When you stand in the center and clap (which we did!) the sound is thunderous. But I think*

Prague was my favorite. It's small and civil and clean and everyone is friendly and unlike most of Europe it's affordable. The fanciest restaurant and you're looking at the menu and it's like 8 crowns. You know, before this year the idea of living outside of the US was unthinkable. I don't consider myself xenophobic but it was just, like, Why? People come TO the US, right? Now I realize that most people in the world aren't even thinking about the US. That they have their cultures and language and practices and ways of living and these are just as good as ours. Sometimes better." Email from my son during year in France.

7. Olga Khazan, "In One Year, 57,375 Years of Life Were Lost to Police Violence," *The Atlantic,* 8 May 2018, https://www.theatlantic.com/health/archive/2018/05/the-57375-years-of-life-lost-to-police-violence/559835/ (accessed 9 Aug. 2018).

8. I saw a bumper sticker once which read: Motherhood: A Noble Profession. I've written about this before, in my book *Divorce Dog: Men, Motherhood and Midlife.*

WOMANISH

1. Rebecca E,pstein, Jamilia J. Blake, Thalia GONZÁLEZ, "Girlhood Interrupted: The Erasure of Black Girls' Childhood," Center on Poverty and Inequality, Georgetown Law, http://www.law.georgetown.edu/academics/centers-institutes/poverty-inequality/upload/girlhood-interrupted.pdf (accessed 15 Aug. 2018).